The Mindful Pianist

Focus, practise, perform, engage

Mark Tanner

Produced and distributed by

FABER *ff* MUSIC

PUBLISHING SERVICES

ISBN10: 0-571-53963-7
EAN13: 978-0-571-53963-5

Contents

for Gily

Foreword

Much has been written about the piano over the years. It seems that it holds a particular fascination for people of all ages and cultures. Ever popular, it now seems to have acquired a new status with avid followers and subscribers to glossy piano magazines. There's no shortage of articles about aspects of repertoire, details of examinations, piano courses, places to study, how to practise, or the latest prize winners. With the ascendency of the Internet, there is now a global marketplace where teachers and pianists compete for attention, eager to promote their wares.

The fact is that, at a basic level, the piano is one of the easiest instruments to play. You don't have to put it in your mouth and blow it, nor do you have to bow it; unfortunately, you don't even have to tune it. Provided the mechanism works, a hammer will do the job for you, and all you have to do is strike the next key. Simple – but of course it then becomes more complicated as reluctant fingers refuse to obey mental commands. Then the habits creep in; the weary acceptance of the same old mistakes, the correcting in the moment, the lack of pulse, the tyranny of ornaments, the lazy pedalling. Working in this way tends to become loud, repetitious and impatient. Far from making 'perfect', this kind of abusive practice makes 'permanent'. As a last resort, the floundering pianist develops a kind of 'wishful listening'; this edits out all the mistakes leaving only the fantasy of performing at the Wigmore Hall on the verge of a standing ovation.

Gordon Green, with whom I had the good fortune to study, used to refer to the 'craft of practising'. He likened the pianist to a master joiner with his box of tools, sharpened and oiled. As the joiner adds to the collection of tools over the years, he becomes accustomed to the old favourites but also acquires new ones. In the same way, the pianist has to build up a box of tools to facilitate the process of practising. One has to deal with all those confusing concepts, such as arm weight, and any number of wrists: tense ones, loose ones, high ones, low ones. Then there is the myth of *legato* fingering and many other traditional piano teaching mantras. On top of all this there is the ever-present bogey word: *tension*; a word whose very utterance can exacerbate what it aims to eliminate, and is the cause of misery for generations of pianists. Though all these things have their place, they have become enshrined in a kind of pianistic methodology. The danger is that the enforcement of such rigid principles can cause lifelong damage, psychological and physical. As Egon Petri, the great pianist and teacher, used to say, one has to learn to do things in every way imaginable. I have found this to be a perceptive and wise observation. It is by investing in movement, and exploring ways of achieving a single goal, that one builds up a bank balance of possibilities which will keep tension at bay and ensure comfort and confidence in performing. It is the difference between being physically overdrawn, or in credit.

In *The Mindful Pianist*, distinguished performers and teachers share their insights and experience to encompass a variety of helpful approaches. The reader will discover much practical advice, which will provide a valuable resource for pianists of all ages and abilities. It is to be hoped that it will provoke thought and encourage the aspiring pianist – and indeed the more established player – to question, to think before playing and to express the music fluently and with joy.

Philip Fowke, May 2016

Acknowledgements

I would like to extend my gratitude to 25 prominent pianists and teachers who generously contributed to the book: Philip Fowke, Murray McLachlan, Leslie Howard, John Lenehan, Allan Schiller, Margaret Fingerhut, Madeline Bruser, Richard McMahon, Harry The Piano, Douglas Finch, Nikki Iles, Penelope Roskell, Anthony Williams, Nancy Litten, Lucinda Mackworth-Young, Nadia Lasserson, Kathryn Page, Meurig Thomas, Margaret Murray-McLeod, Frederick Stocken, Melanie Spanswick, Paul Comeau, Melvyn Cooper, Brian Ellsbury and Colin Decio. I remain grateful also to the inestimable number of piano students whom I have had the privilege to learn from over the years, whether at Taunton School in Somerset, where I was Assistant Director of Music for some 16 years, or at an array of adult education establishments and piano summer schools, masterclasses at home and abroad, and of course privately; in their multiplicity of ways, these fleeting connections all added something of concrete value to the book.

I also wish to thank Mary Chandler, Senior Editor at Faber Music, for project managing the book and to Rebecca Castell for editing. Additional proof-reading and, as ever, invaluable help with shaping the overall concept, came from Gillian Poznansky. I also wish to give special thanks to Murray McLachlan, Chair of EPTA, for inviting me to continue the *Piano Professional* series forwards with Faber Music.

I continue to take great pleasure from my work as an examiner, adjudicator and teacher, as well as my appearances as pianist. Alongside these activities I enjoy the richness of experience that comes from working alongside a number of organisations, both at home and abroad. Taken together, this all adds up to a large bank of experiences from which to draw; I should add that, aside from the aforementioned contributions, all of the opinions expressed herein reflect my personal views.

The book was written in its entirety while undertaking a lengthy tour to the Far East in the Spring/Summer of 2016; countless hours spent typing away in the incomparably chaotic coffee shops of Seoul, Osaka and Tokyo brought home to me the vivid reality of being mindfully engaged. I hope the book will intrigue, delight and perhaps even raise the odd eyebrow. The overarching ambition is to help the piano fraternity to meet its rather special role with even greater fortitude, confidence and satisfaction. I also hope it will lend a broader, more tangible sense of perspective to what I suspect is a subject often skimmed over among pianists: doing what we do more mindfully.

Introduction

'Mindfulness' is very much a word of our time – perhaps even *the* word of our time. It implies a quasi-Buddhist stance, with practitioners mastering inner strength, awareness and control via daily mental exercises, as well as the development of meditation and breathing exercises. Not even the more cynical among us could dispute the validity and benefits that mindfulness can bring to pianism, whether for individual players or for piano teachers to impart to students. And yet, until this point, there has been very little written on the subject of mindfulness *specifically* crafted for pianists. Authoritative, confident piano playing at all levels requires reflection, mental control and even some element of meditation (Mark Tanner proposes the term 'practical meditation'). Piano teachers need an awareness of how to encourage this. They need guidance so that they can mentor and stimulate the healthy mental – perhaps even 'spiritual' – development of their students.

Mark Tanner is a modern day polymath who is already well-known to the piano teaching community as a prolific composer and Guest Editor of *Piano Professional* Magazine. His virtuoso playing, experience as an examiner, teacher, and interest in culture generally, place him ideally to tackle mindfulness for pianists and piano teachers. This highly concentrated, challenging and illuminating guide is full of lateral thinking and common sense, as well as canny artistic and intellectual observations. It is thought-provoking and stimulating, way beyond its relatively modest dimensions. By this, I mean that the ideas and concepts the book so beautifully introduces will grow and develop in readers as they continue to reflect upon and bring these ideas into daily practice. The guest contributions, from so many esteemed colleagues in the piano-playing world, which have been generously dispersed throughout the text, add colour and anecdote, as well as further weight and insight.

The Mindful Pianist is the third book in the ongoing *Piano Professional* series of books published by Faber Music in association with EPTA UK, following on logically and naturally from its first two books: *The Foundations of Technique* and *Piano Technique in Practice*. All three publications will be seen as relevant and useful to teachers and pianists of all ages, levels and motivations. EPTA UK is extremely grateful to Mark Tanner for penning what is unquestionably a highly inspiring, yet practical and down-to-earth book.

Murray McLachlan, June 2016

Part 1

Focussing

1 Mindfulness in music

Beyond the mysticism

Mindfulness has captured the public's imagination in a giddying array of ways during recent times. Though its origins lie in Buddhist meditation, modern thinkers have been quick to recognise the potential for improving our psychological well-being via activities as diverse as sport, macramé and even bread-making. Hence in this broader, secular sense, mindfulness has acquired a non-spiritual emphasis. It acknowledges the need for inner calm and self-reflection – indeed a more wholesome awareness of how we go about our daily lives. The Mental Health Foundation endorses the cultivation of mindfulness, and this has found practical outlets in institutions prone to claustrophobia and anxiety disorders, such as correctional institutions, learning places and even multinational companies.

Tuning in to our potential, both as pianists and in our everyday lives, requires us to take a bold step away from the distractions which insidiously permeate our existence. Our preoccupation with competition and ambition leads us, often unwittingly, into a dizzying world of haste, breathlessness and confusion. Attempts to regroup all too soon leave us feeling we are underachieving again. There is nothing new about stress of course, but today we do battle with neurosis on an unprecedented scale. The tyranny of email and social media may partly account for this sense of being weighed down by scrutiny and accountability. Furthermore, we have become overburdened by choice; the very freedom to wander easily around our global village requires us to reject options which under other circumstances we might feel are ideally suited to us. It is undoubtedly easier to choose between a dozen options than one million and, ironically, it seems that keeping our options open for too long merely increases the risk of making none.

The average twenty-five-year-old has already notched up adventures abroad which knock the experiences of their parents into a cocked hat. But they too are feeling the strain of a society which has left them in the lurch; they are unsure whether to be enchanted or terrified by their future. Our sometimes uneasy society, struggling to come to terms with its ever-shifting identity, is leading us inexorably towards a 'dabble-culture'. We are left feeling unfulfilled as we dip in and out of activities, piano playing sometimes among these, any one of which could soak up a whole lifetime. Our shelves groan under the weight of unread books, while the simple satisfaction of walking among the flowers seems inevitably interrupted by the beeping of our smartphones, alerting us to what is trending on Twitter. We measure our day not by what we may have achieved, but with the numbing suspicion that we ought to have accomplished more.

One irony here is that even those areas of our lives which should be able to draw us away from our daily tensions can so easily succumb, too. Take piano playing for example, an activity which has the power to turn us from avid music-lovers into disillusioned practitioners, frustrated by our pace of progress and unsure how to move forward. Our need to find a way of fulfilling ourselves, even in our leisure activities, has reached an unprecedented high, for work and play seem inextricably melded together as never before.

Exercising mindfulness in music can help us to confront the throb of discontentment with renewed confidence and directness. It is an approach to reigniting the spirit of optimism which we all urgently need to sustain us as enthusiastic musicians. Mindfulness takes as its starting point the delightfully uncomplicated idea that we can ultimately find fulfilment within ourselves. Through activities designed to reconnect us with our instrument, our minds and our bodies, we find ourselves falling in love with our musical personas all over again. In evolving our sensory awareness, we can channel our energies where their impact will be greatest.

Understanding *why* we are perhaps progressing more slowly than we wish is the first step to becoming mindful and prosperous in our piano playing. We can all be shown how to optimise our practising – a significant point given that time has become one of our most precious commodities. Knowing how to build performances we can be proud of will enable us to pick up the pace and become once again exhilarated by what we are able to achieve with our instrument. Rekindling a spirit of curiosity for the music we have grown stale practising is not someone else's responsibility, it is ours. From here we can contemplate the challenges in new pieces with unbridled vigour and excitement.

The complex simplicity of piano playing

From day one, it seems pianists are predestined to inhabit a parallel universe. In contrast with flautists or violinists, who will commonly experience the thrill and camaraderie of ensemble playing of some kind from early on in their studies, we pianists must learn to fend for ourselves. Pianists miss out on the invaluable sectional practice and time-management skills which conductors and choir directors instil in rehearsals. They have no idea what it is to spend protracted periods counting umpteen bars of rests while music detonates into life from all around them, only then to be reprimanded for not threading into the texture with sufficient sensitivity. The pianist's bubble-like existence permits him or her to start, stop, stutter and stall with blissful disregard to the emerging musical landscape. Hence an ability to maintain a really solid beat, to listen intently and take account of someone else's vision for the music, will likely be facets of playing less intuitively ingrained into the pianist's psyche. Among a host of other vital social and musical skills, an ability to sight-read frequently slips off the list, too.

No amount of working in isolation can ever make up for these lost hours of corporate learning, listening and music-making, though it seems we feel we can compensate by working harder and for longer in tiny light-starved rooms. By necessity, wind and brass players must learn to be more time-savvy when practising – after all, they cannot grind away hour upon hour as the pianist might.

As a result, pianists rely almost exclusively on brief encounters with teachers for support, guidance and orientation. Even if it is possible to teach pianists in groups effectively, it will never be possible for them to *practise* collectively in quite the way other instrumentalists and singers take for granted. Only those who are able to strike a healthy balance between self-praise and self-criticism, effort expended and advantage gained, will be successful in their own terms. From the first tentative gestures at the instrument the pianist's psychology and personal journey will necessarily be somewhat out of kilter with their fellow musicians. Realistically, aside from duet playing, pianists usually become useful members of the wider musical community only once they have reached a relatively advanced level, by which time a clarinettist of comparable accomplishment may well have performed in dozens of youth orchestra concerts and evolved a natural affinity with what it means to be a functioning musician – importantly, wind, brass and string players already value themselves as members of a 'winning team'.

Admittedly, there are schools of thought, Suzuki notable among these, which actively encourage the support of parents in a commendable bid to nurture the younger pianist, while at the same time counter the problem of insularity by introducing ensemble playing from Kindergarten age. Furthermore, in the West especially there has been a sea-change in approach to school group keyboard learning in recent times, which may conceivably improve the situation for adult players in years to come. Nevertheless, for the vast majority of adult players today, the loneliness of the long-distance pianist tacitly prevails, and it may not be overstating the case to suggest that the mental well-being of pianists is frequently put in jeopardy. The traditional view, that pianists thrive upon intense periods of solitude, driven slavishly by an ambition for self-improvement, seems highly questionable as a blanket philosophy; alas, like it or not, solitude will always be intrinsic to the pianist's lot.

Ideally, anything that we practise in our lives ought to resonate readily with the experience itself – think of how we typically learn to drive or swim, for example. But in this sense, from a pianist's viewpoint, the act of performance could hardly be more different. Can it really be surprising that hang-ups among adult pianists so frequently dislodge their confidence to perform in front of others?

I am sure we can all relate to the following scenario.

Saturday morning, 11:30

We approach the new day's practice session brimming with optimism and expectation. As usual, we start out with a few fragmentary ideas of how to proceed, partly drawing from the previous day's experience.

We know exactly what needs tackling, for our teacher has spelled it out plainly enough, and besides, there is a diploma bearing down on us in the middle distance, which is having an inordinate impact on the current workload. It is as if every finger needs to be woken up individually, though at first it is not clear whether the brain is instructing the fingers or the other way around. Although feeling a little creaky at first, there are encouraging glimpses of where we are headed. From the pile of books next to us we spot conspicuous evidence of unfinished business – unlearned studies, unpolished sonatas and unconscionable concertos. The task ahead weighs heavily; nevertheless we sharpen our focus and begin the session by tackling that knotty leap in bar 174 of the Rachmaninov. It's not becoming any easier, nor has it been for the past few days, in fact it might even be a little worse for all the attention it's been getting. We gaze out through the window and spot the neighbour's cat snoozing on the birdbath and sigh, before glancing down at our mobile phone in the hope of semi-legitimate distraction.

Back to the leap, or rather, the crash, for only one in five attempts succeeds at hitting that wretched G♯. Frustrated now, we find fault with the dog-eared page, which has acquired a will of its own, fluttering maddeningly in response to every minuscule breeze. The sunlight shining on the page has maliciously begun to obliterate the lines of music we are attempting to play. It's all too much to bear; time for a coffee…

…Discontented with how things seem to be progressing, we flick forward to a place in the score with which we feel a little more comfortable and launch ourselves manfully at it. This is one section we ought to be managing pretty well by now, and yet hurdles aplenty seem to have newly installed themselves overnight. We've been going hammer and tongs at it for perhaps twenty minutes now, and there seems little to show for the effort expended. Undaunted, we gear up for a full run-through, optimistic that a degree of momentum or divine intervention will occur, if only to repay our dogged determination. Inevitably, the run slows steadily to a canter and culminates as a feeble limp to the finishing line. It's one-nil to Rachmaninov, but we have emerged with a little dignity intact, and besides, there's always tomorrow. A quick peek at the mobile and it's time to be thinking about lunch. Thank goodness for that.

Even longer-toothed pianists regularly encounter this kind of hapless scenario, where an optimistic outlook rapidly degenerates into a profitless panic, irritation and dissatisfaction. We end up merely confirming the insuperability of the difficulty, not overcoming it. The problem is that we become solely concerned with slaying our pianistic demons and fail to take account of what we need as human beings. We all thrive on positive feedback, and this includes the words of approval we mutter silently to ourselves as we toil away. Regular growth-spurts, albeit measured with a micrometre rather than a ruler, are indispensable stepping-stones to maintaining a positive psychology, for we pianists are anything but indestructible. We have learned that repetition is key to ingraining muscular memory, and yet we overlook the need to triangulate our efforts, i.e. to come at each problem systematically and via different directions. Trumpeters know that the best way to strike high notes with confidence is to practise lots of low ones, but pianists tend to lose heart when a one-dimensional approach fails to yield immediate rewards.

We underestimate the importance of stopping to digest what is going wrong. Even a few seconds' hiatus between repetitions would greatly add to what is being gained from all this physical working out. After all, eliminating what does not work is a vital step towards honing a strategy that will. Besides, we are not robots – we need time to reappraise, time to restore faith in ourselves, time to recover and move on. We learn little from the energy spent and instead enter a pernicious, ever-tightening loop of negativity: the harder we try, the more invincible the problem seems, and as our playing steadily deteriorates, so does our composure and our resolve. We unwittingly get faster and faster at each repetition and narrow the gaps between futile attempts in a wholly counterproductive cycle. We soon grow accustomed to underachieving as we learn to trade progress for high blood-pressure, satisfaction for anguish. It is almost as though we can justify a pedestrian pace of improvement by acknowledging how worn out and stressed we have become: *no pain, no gain*. This machismo may sustain us for many years, camouflaging granular improvement and hoodwinking us into thinking we are doing all that is feasible.

You may or may not have caught a glimpse of yourself somewhere in this scenario; the good news is that by making subtle adjustments to our approach we may successfully pull ourselves free from all this meaningless flagellation and begin an entirely new, progressive learning journey that will sustain us for the rest of our lives.

Even professional pianists need to regroup from time to time and question why they are not advancing at the rate they would wish.[1] One rather eminent British pianist's repertoire was, by his own admission, so slim upon reaching success in the Leeds Competition, that he slipped into something of a blind panic when attempting to live up to all the hyped expectation; he knew he would have to step up to the plate in order to sustain the feverish pace of international concert giving. His is a story few music students would have little difficulty empathising with. In my late teens, it was as if I had all the time in the world to learn and memorise large-scale pieces. Consequently, I took my time and became used to functioning at a sedate, unhurried pace. I recall spending near enough an entire year getting two sizeable works under my fingers: Ravel's

1 The term 'self-compassion', coined by the American Educational Psychologist, Kristin Neff, fifteen years ago, came in response to a perceived 'unhealthy attitude to oneself', a syndrome especially prevalent among senior-ranking musicians. (Kristin Neff, cited in Kageyama N., March 2016: *PAN, Journal of the British Flute Society*, 38–41.) Typically speaking, the 'Type A' personality is characterised as their own worst enemy – highly self-critical and comparatively unable to celebrate their own successes. Such personalities may lean towards hypertension and are also inclined to react badly to perceived shortcomings or suggestions of inadequacy.

Gaspard de la Nuit and Beethoven's Fourth Piano Concerto, whereas I would like to think I would function at three times the pace nowadays.

Years later, when I was teaching full-time and simultaneously trying to sustain both a performing career and research for a PhD, my mindset altered radically. The occasional forty minutes of dead time gifted to me by an absent pupil became something to be prized. Paradoxically, it rapidly dawned on me that my rate of learning and memorising had increased exponentially. I hadn't become any more pianistically adept overnight, simply more mindful and resourceful with my time. This realisation sparked a turning point in my entire attitude to working, both at the piano and away from it, which led to the approach I have subsequently taken in my teaching.

Many of the ideas in this book stem naturally from this epiphanic period, for I have come to understand that the role of the teacher is to teach pupils how to teach themselves. Thought of in this way, every practice session becomes a self-taught lesson, and as a consequence the rate of gain immeasurably outstrips the 'slog till you drop' philosophy – the bane of many an underachieving pianist.

Piano playing as a practical meditation

There is comfort to be found in the execution of simple household tasks. The physical effort expended in filling a wheelbarrow with grass cuttings leaves little energy for troubling over the state of your share portfolio – in a sense, the more menial the task, the better suited it is to providing a distraction, albeit short-lived. Controversially perhaps, for many people, playing the piano fulfils a not dissimilar purpose. The act of focussing on, say, improving left-hand evenness in a Clementi Sonatina, may force us to relax our grip on an entirely unrelated personal problem which, left unchecked, may have nagged away unwittingly into other aspects of our day. The problem with our minds is not so much the negative thoughts which invade us just when we were beginning to make a bit of progress with our piano playing, but the anguish we put ourselves through immediately afterwards. In other words, do we choose to acknowledge a temporary failing – unevenness, a few wrong notes, a slightly unsteady pulse – and continue forwards undeterred with a plan of action, or reprimand ourselves for our shortcomings?

> It is said in the East that 'you become what you meditate on'. Playing the piano, or more specifically, playing music on the piano, is a way of meditating on sound, and by extension, *becoming* the sound. When music truly flows, there is a wonderful feeling of emersion, a true lack of self. The music plays itself and the composer's voice is heard. So we, as performers, have to get out of the way of the music in order for it to be truly heard. This requires the disciplining of attention; in a word, *concentration*.[2] **Colin Decio**

2 In an interview with Justin Goulding of BBC Sport, cricketer Alastair Cook, England's record Test run-scorer (who as a boy sang at St Paul's Cathedral School) said: 'The musical training taught me to focus my mind, before playing in an orchestra taught me how to truly concentrate'.

While piano playing can alleviate unrelated problems which crop up in our day, it may itself become the problem as we set about practising. For example, the perceived uneven left hand in the aforementioned Clementi may unwittingly raise doubts over the right hand's securities on the next page, and from here we start to trouble over whether the tempo is really rock-solid in that busy sequential build-up near the end. Our proclivity for self-doubting – as distinct from profitable self-questioning – can leave us feeling angry; we end up wondering whether our technical limitations will ever permit anything of quality to emerge from our efforts. These are perfectly natural thoughts, but they are also counterproductive. An experienced piano teacher will not consider a lesson to have been an utter washout if a pupil fails to achieve immediate mastery of a particular aspect, for they have learned to expect such things to trickle slowly into their pupil's mind and fingers; rather, their task is to implant the seeds of good practice, then trust the pupil to work through the difficulties one by one. The pupil, on the other hand, is rarely so patient or forgiving of him/herself, and this is where a disproportionate escalation of one's negative mental state can occur over the longer term.

By being shown how to focus on the music we are making – not the issues we face in trying to eradicate flaws – we can effectively 'reboot' the mind. Every day we need to fall in love with the piano all over again, and this act of being generous with ourselves in pursuit of an immediate, attainable reward, is our route out of the maze. The practicality of playing, and of sensing what our creative impulses actually sound like, therefore amounts to a practical meditation. Thought of in this way, repetitions in our practising become more mindful and genuinely useful, not debilitating loops which merely draw attention to what we do not seem able to do.

> Something I find helps me to 'enter the zone' when practising – either working on a piece of repertoire or improvising – is to allow myself to listen right through to the ends of notes. As pianists, I think we concentrate most of our energy on producing the sound by way of our initial contact with the keys, and we then tend to let the sound go its own way without really hearing what happens next. As an improvisation exercise, I ask my students to close their eyes, put the pedal down, randomly drop their hands onto the keys and then listen to the chord right through to the very end of its gradual decay, trying to hear what happens to the sound along the way. This process of decay is not so straightforward and linear as many of us imagine. The panoply of sympathetic vibrations and harmonics is so rich and multifarious that allowing ourselves to experience it, unencumbered by duty and guilt, helps us regain the pleasurable and non-judgemental feeling of hearing what it is we are playing. **Douglas Finch**

2 The pragmatic pianist

Feeling comfortable in our own skin

In an ideal world we can all manage Rachmaninov's 13th stretch without breaking a sweat. On this same utopian planet, we retain the use of all joints and muscles until we become centenarians (after all, Arthur Rubinstein carried on giving public performances until the ripe old age of 89).[3] In the real world, a somewhat contrasting picture emerges. We may encounter the first signs of joint ache in our forties, start to feel just a little jaded about our intellectual powers before we have reached 60, and have slowly receded from the status of 'piano hero' aged 20 into an irascible 50-year-old experiencing twinges of wrist ache just from carrying in the supermarket shopping.

With a little help, somewhere between these two (admittedly puerile) extremes awaits the real 'us', comfortable in our own skin and confident in our mental fortitude. We have become reconciled to our frailties and more mindful of our qualities. We now weigh up the piano music we would still dearly love to play against repertoire more suited to our physical frame and mental capacities. We take pleasure in doing the 'simple' things well in our piano playing, and rejoice in the immeasurable satisfaction of hearing ourselves play shorter, less taxing pieces rather well. We esteem our musical maturity more highly than we once did and treasure the doors it opens for us when playing the simplest phrase. We have realised that two hours well spent (and preferably split in half by a good seven hours) does us so much more good than the six hours we once were convinced might turn us into Murray Perahia. We have sensibly adjusted our sitting position to accommodate the lower backache we get if we sit too high.[4] Indeed, we have begun to treat our bodies more sympathetically, not as though they are made of plasticine. We have learned to esteem the sound of our instrument as highly as any torrent of notes, and gradually invest our hard-won life experience gainfully into our music-making.

Our ambitions have become centred on those aspects of playing which reward us the most pleasure and now live more confidently in our emotional world, delighting in making music which simply makes its point and moves on. We resolve not to overreach ourselves in pursuit of the unachievable, but instead enjoy the simple glory of a beautifully-voiced chord or an impeccably hewn melody. We have learned to 'park' our inhibitions somewhere where they are less harmful to us, and celebrate our new-found ability to bring pleasure to others. We have also come to appreciate many different kinds of silence, not just in the music we love to play but in the natural world around us, and become more sensually connected with the piano as an organic extension of ourselves.

3 Arthur Rubinstein (1887–1982), a Polish-American pianist considered by many to be the greatest exponent of Chopin's music of his day.
4 www.alexandertechnique.com

We now feel more alive to the possibilities presented by alternative approaches in our piano playing; we have even resolved to venture off-piste a little more often. We have learned to adapt to our physiological imperfections and to embrace the changes in our bodies and minds with serenity.

Mindful meddling

Arriving at this easy relationship with ourselves as pianists may require us to make bold, occasionally contentious decisions. When we lack the immediate facility to tackle a leap in Liszt or a stretch in Chopin we need to be on the lookout for plausible workarounds. This is not a question of whether we should compromise the integrity of a piece of music, more a matter of common sense. We wouldn't balk at the suggestion to put insoles in our loose shoes, and yet it always baffles me when fellow pianists or teachers take a snooty view of making pragmatic changes to piano music. These might include taking a chord in the other hand when helpful – the opening phrase of Schoenberg's Suite Op.19 No.4 becomes inestimably easier when the notated *forte* right-hand chord is taken in the left hand.[5] Or it might mean daring to 'reimagine' a chord-voicing, leaving out a doubled-up note in the left hand, or else arpeggiating[6] the odd chord to make possible a piece which would otherwise remain tantalisingly beyond reach.[7] Adverse reactions to the very idea of using the pedal to alleviate an awkward corner in a Bach fugue are surprisingly common, and it is by no means only older pianists who might take such an ascetic view – teenage players can at times be amusingly judgemental when it comes to matters of judicious 'meddling'.

My view is that most of us are fortunate enough to have ten digits and two feet with which to meet the often considerable demands of the music we are playing; an unwillingness to make maximum use of our resources seems questionably abstemious. We see how ingenious pianists with disabilities can be when forced to reinvent their technique following a tragic illness or accident. Cyril Smith had to overcome the lost mobility of his left arm following a stroke, and there are quite a few other examples of pianists who have had to make similar compromises.[8]

For a bet, I once spent an entire day at music college attempting to play Mendelssohn's *Andante and Rondo Capriccioso* without using my thumbs – it proved immensely challenging, technically nigh on impossible unless taken at a quarter speed, and hence not something I am planning to do again anytime soon. But it certainly proved to me (as if proof were needed) how useful those

---

5 Schoenberg's Suite Op.19, No.4, *Rash, aber leicht*, bar 2, demisemiquaver chord: F and B.
6 In the opening chords to Rachmaninov's Second Concerto, Vladimir Ashkenazy wisely elects to arpeggiate.
7 'Harpsichord playing traditionally used a great deal of arpeggiation. Even when the fortepiano superseded the harpsichord, performers would naturally play the newer instrument in the same way as the old one' (Stevenson R., 1992: *The Paderewski Paradox*, p.13).
8 Cyril Smith (1909–1974), a British pianist who became widely known for his interpretations of Rachmaninov, Schubert and Chopin. He married Phyllis Sellick, a fellow pianist and professor at the Royal College of Music. Having reinvented himself as one-third of a three-handed duo following an attack of thrombosis in the Ukraine in 1956, Smith and Sellick went on to achieve considerable fame.

weird appendages flapping around on our hands really are.[9] The more flexible we are when we tackle piano music, and the more willing to investigate the possibility of sensible solutions to commonly encountered difficulties, the better chance we stand of being able to do what we are trying to do – and this ought to be incentive enough.

While some of our pianistic challenges stem from the demands made by the composer – Liszt was no slouch in this regard – others are really only there because of their appearance within the score. Just because an editor, or indeed the composer himself, happens to have chosen to place certain notes in the bass clef, when they could just as sensibly have been written in the treble clef, or vice versa, it is not an irrefutable decision. Take the opening to Liszt's Consolation No.3 for example, where the right hand can take a little pressure off the left if need be, not just at the beginning, but later on too, or indeed in a fair amount of Gershwin's music, notably the Prelude No.2, where a similar set of possibilities await discovery.

Liszt, Consolation No. 3, bb. 1–2

Gershwin, Prelude No. 2, bb. 1–2

The middle pedal is surely among the pragmatic pianist's most overlooked resources, especially when tackling repertoire from around 1800 (indeed half a century before the 'sostenuto' was first officially unveiled at the French Industrial Exposition), and where there are issues of small hand-size. With it, you might consider catching an occasional octave (or even a single note here and there) in the bass, and then expeditiously playing notes elsewhere higher up the instrument a nanosecond later; this can be great fun incidentally, even if you happen to have hands the size of dinner plates.[10] Another excellent example would be the opening chords in Debussy's *La Cathédrale engloutie* where, in combination with the sustain pedal, we can have the best of both worlds: an emphatic 'pedal' note and majestic organ-like chords sounding out with pristine clarity.

9　The marvellous painting entitled 'Lady Seated at a Virginal', by the Dutch artist Johannes Vermeer (painted between 1670 and 1672) shows how prim ladies of the day refrained from using the thumbs when playing the virginal.

10　It would be worth taking a look at Liszt's transcription of Bach's Prelude and Fugue in C major BSV 544–S462/2, where right-hand semiquavers need to bat along at some speed while a 'pedal' note grumbles menacingly in the subterranean register.

Debussy, *La Cathédrale engloutie*, bb. 28–30

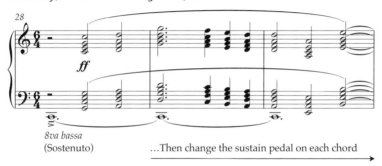

If you experiment regularly with the middle pedal you too can become a veritable Gene Kelly of pedalling, deftly sliding the right foot from the *sostenuto* to the sustain pedal, and back again, while perhaps simultaneously using the left foot to operate the *una corda* and then take its turn with the *sostenuto*! There seems little point in pianists becoming expert at sleight-of-hand if we are going to neglect the possibility of becoming fleet-of-foot also.

If we dare to think 'outside the box', we can sometimes come up with cunning ways of sidestepping irksome issues that would remain unresolved by a more conventional route. By way of example, in Ravel's 'Ondine', from *Gaspard de la Nuit*, we need to hear a crystal-clear but softly-spoken statement of the water nymph's tune, just after the tumultuous cascade of notes at bar 89. This is virtually impossible to achieve using the sustain pedal, or even *sostenuto*. This is because this beautiful, plaintive melody must somehow emerge from a 'backwash' of colour ringing on from the previous flourish, which has been trapped in the pedal. An unconventional solution lies in placing the entire left hand (and even forearm) onto the notes in the middle register to silently depress some keys *after* the pedalled flourish has taken place. We can then slowly lift the sustain pedal, thereby transferring much of the backwash away from the foot to the arm: we can now take all the time we wish 'painting' this exquisite melody, entirely free from unwanted blurring and with the flourish still reverberating hauntingly – voila!

Ravel, 'Ondine', from *Gaspard de la Nuit*, bb. 89–93

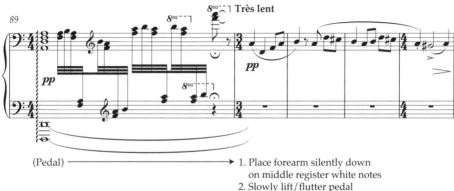

The importance of making mastikes

I once attended a masterclass in which a friend of mine performed Prokofiev's Sixth Sonata; he achieved a manic characterisation the like of which I have yet to hear rivalled. Everyone present was in some way impressed with the playing, despite its fair share of smudges and splashes, for it had terrific drive and commitment. Curiously, and regrettably in my opinion, we all heard the maestro mutter under his breath as he rose from his seat, 'well, there were enough wrong notes in this performance to create an entirely new piece...'. It does seem a pity that we so quickly seize upon the deficiencies in piano playing before turning our minds to the enviable dynamism that may have been achieved. Accepting a degree of latitude in note accuracy is important for the majority of us under certain circumstances – most of us *will* play wrong notes, and that is a fact, so we would be best-advised to acknowledge these as they crop up, much as an actor must sidestep over stumbled words occasionally and strive not to jeopardise the grander theatrical moment.

If we attempt to 'correct' a mistake in a performance, the net result is a second, arguably more noticeable error, for the second error merely draws attention to the first. Moreover, our best attempts to eradicate wrong notes tend to shut down our willingness to take risks, so that the net result becomes a hermetically-sealed, emotionally flaccid performance.[11] Wrong notes are not the end of the world, though arguably a boring performance comes a little closer to being so. I once heard a well-known Russian pianist greet his protégé pupil after a rather anarchic recital of Liszt's *Transcendental Studies*: 'You played like a *terrorist*'. My friend turned to me and sighed, 'better than playing like a chartered accountant'.

An insightful article by the American Musicologist, Andrew Adams, highlights the need for us to be a little kinder to ourselves regarding mistakes, and indeed to be more circumspect about what we think of as constituting an error.[12] If we play a note that is not written, i.e. confusing it for another, this amounts to a misreading, not a mistake *per se* – after all, it was intentional, not an accident – whereas if we try to strike the 'right' note, but fail to do so, surely this would be better described as a mis-hit. But how about a breach of harmony caused by ineffective pedalling, a less-than-evenly dispatched running passage, or a persistently bumpy thumb in scale playing? What about deficient balance or a dearth of dynamic shape – are these not 'mistakes', too? As Adams sensibly reflects, we ought to be clearer about the language we use when we are in the throes of maligning ourselves or others about perceived deficiencies or inaccuracies.

It seems the more elevated the stature of the pianist, the more elevated the nature of the mistakes they may be likely to encounter. An architectural faux-pas (for example, not awarding sufficient presence to an important motif reappearing in the recapitulation of a sonata) might score relatively low on the Richter scale of mistake-making, but only if you happen to be the kind of

---

11 On the other hand, a pianist does not take risks simply to entertain – there has to be a desire to impress *oneself*.
12 Adams A., Winter 2015, Issue 40: 'Johannes, Pull Yourself Together: Exploring the Inner World of Errors, Anger and Self-Talk', in *Piano Professional*, Ed. Tanner M., 5–7.

pianist who meets with more basic blunders on a regular basis. A top-flight pianist might become frustrated in a recording session if intended subtleties are not emerging quite as anticipated, but these perceived shortcomings will surely be every bit as hard to bear as blatant 'wrong-uns' from the fingers of a more modest player.

Renowned pianists of yesteryear – Arthur Schnabel being a prime example[13] – would appear to have had a different attitude to mistakes entirely, as Madeline Bruser cautioned me when I interviewed her at her studio in New York last year for *Piano Professional*.[14] For it was the *spirit* of the music that was of chief importance to pianists in those first few decades of the 20th century – the power to communicate something of lasting musical value; hence lapses in accuracy tended to be received rather more charitably and shrugged off as minor collateral damage.

There are those mistakes which we can reasonably hope to avoid by learning the music really thoroughly in the first place – notes and rhythms would certainly fall into this category – but equally there will be aspects of playing, such as hand-coordination, balance, evenness of touch and so on, which surely come under a quite different heading. Whatever you may personally think warrants the term 'mistake', be sure to learn from them wherever possible; mistakes form an indispensable, even enjoyable part of improving. We usually learn more when things go wrong, or at least when we are made aware that things are not quite as they should be. Without mistakes there can be no possibility for growing in self-awareness or coming to a realisation about how to move forward in our playing. Mistakes open our teachers' eyes and ears to where we are going wrong, and this is precisely what we are paying them to do. Mistakes are also the clues we ourselves can learn to pick up on as we practise mindfully at home alone.

One potential problem when it comes to weighing up the impact of mistakes in our piano playing, is that we easily overreact to their presence instead of according them a positive purpose. The trial-and-error philosophy holds good in many circumstances – first we test ourselves, perhaps with a new fingering or hand shape, but we immediately see its limited value, so we make a small adjustment and persevere. Students sometimes give off the impression that there is some kind of conspiracy going on inside them, a malevolent force willing them to fail out of pure spite as they endeavour to play. This kind of internal warfare is both dispiriting, tedious, and ultimately just a waste of valuable energy.

Overreacting can take many forms, but they each undermine and confuse us in ways which can inflict lasting damage. In a masterclass, for example, we might be told that our touch is too frail, that we are not key-bedding sufficiently well.

---

13 Arthur Schnabel (1882–1951). An Austrian pianist of supreme intellect, Schnabel remains an enduring fascination for today's younger generations of pianists; he was a musician who despised showmanship and preferred to make his mark with penetrating performances, notably of the Beethoven and Schubert Sonatas.
14 A most profitable read: Bruser, M., 1997: *The Art of Practising: A Guide to Making Music from the Heart* (New York, Three Rivers Press/Crown Publishing).

For the next two years we proceed to attack the keys like a crazed octopus, rendering every perfumed phrase in our Fauré Nocturnes like one of the more vehement passages from a Prokofiev Concerto.[15] Worse still, we may make ill-conceived adjustments to our interpretation or technique while we are actually *playing*, thus confusing ourselves and rendering the experience highly unsettling for the listener. For this reason, when I am giving masterclasses I usually encourage the student to have one or two goes at something new, then smile and tell them to take my idea away them and work it through rationally, away from the heat. Aim to reach an understanding with your mistakes, else they may continue to rise up and bite you on the nose for the rest of your life.

Remembering to forget what we have learned

There is clearly a middle ground between responding to the sensory experience of playing a piano piece and analysing the living daylights out of it. Inevitably, as lifelong students of our instrument we probably find ourselves doing some of each on a regular basis. First, we listen, enjoy, sigh, smile or grimace, and a moment later, perhaps subconsciously, we consider what it was, either in the performance or the piece itself, that appears to make it tick. Granted, some of us gravitate more naturally towards one mode or the other, but there is a danger that the more interested in the nuts and bolts of piano music we become, the less instinctively aware we may be of the music's capacity to stir an emotional response from us.

It is almost as though we need to forget what we have learned in order to access this more fundamental, primeval response to the music, much as a chef might do when sitting down to eat in someone else's restaurant. Composers, in the main, do not write pieces to edify so much as to enjoy, and we pianists should not regard ourselves as beyond reach merely because we are charged with coaxing the piece into life. If we are not pleasing ourselves we can hardly be pleasing others, and yet I find it frequently to be the case that pianists forget to listen with the same ferocity of determination as members of their audience may be doing. Perhaps it is because we have so many notes to play that we inadvertently shut down the ears and rely on the fingers to pay attention on our behalf, or maybe we have not been shown how best to go about it. Later in the book I will be touching on what it is to be a 'virtuoso listener', and there is nothing tongue-in-cheek about the position I am encouraging pianists to take here. In the meantime, there is a great deal we can do in pursuit of our former 'naivety' and to reacquaint our ears with the resplendent sound of the piano – surely, the very sensation which caused us to fall in love with the instrument in the first place.

The first approach is so blindingly obvious most of us never really give it serious consideration. Make a point of playing through some very easy pieces each day – music you know inside out and can practically play in your sleep

15 Prokofiev fervently rejected the idea that any of his music – even the magnificent *Suggestion Diabolique* and *Sarcasms* – was in any way 'grotesque', despite assertions from various quarters.

(we should all have a reservoir of such pieces).[16] This will permit you to look away from the piano while you are playing. If you prefer, improvise, but don't get too busy with your fingers, just soak up the sound and wallow in it like an elephant at a watering hole. As well as enabling us to relax and simply 'play', more importantly this activity instantly confers responsibility to the ears, fingers and feet (note, *not* the eyes) for gauging what is pleasurable. The tactility of playing is just as rewarding a sensation as the sonic effect on our eardrums, and our feet too can absorb a surprising amount of resonance, especially if we take off our shoes and socks.

Conversely, when we read from a score, our eyes eagerly devour the dots and squiggles. The scatter-bomb of information commonly results in mixed success – some of it effectively flags up what is musically possible and/or desirable, but an appreciable amount is simply lost in translation and seems to accumulate like fuzz on a draft excluder. Paradoxically, the better we are at assimilating the black stuff flying about the page (and hence the clearer the line of communication between the eyes and the fingers), the more prone to shutting off our other senses we seem to become. In other words, we may rely so heavily upon our bullet-proof reading ability that we pay comparatively little heed to the sound that is actually emanating from the instrument. The sense of oneness we can achieve from playing simple piano music with utter commitment to the quality of the sound is indescribable. This observation is perhaps especially pertinent to the more advanced pianist who habitually finds him/herself under siege from an avalanche of notes and is at risk of detachment from the instrument's chief sensual attribute.

Sound: The jewel in the crown of expert piano playing

> One's focus ideally should be on the musical 'conversation', not the technique. However, time spent grappling with fingerings, notes, chords, ornaments, tempo marks, memory and all the rest of it, can easily mean 'sound' is last in the queue. The infinite variety of colours and inflections a fine instrument can produce are miraculous. Relaxed, non-tense muscles (everywhere but the fingertips) are, for me, a precondition, but curiously, an equally important first step might also be conceptual. When you want to produce a particular sound – beautiful or otherwise – imagine it first and, most importantly, listen for it; seek it out!
> Richard McMahon

Pianists could learn a great deal from sitting outside a professional flautist's practice room for half an hour. I live with one, so I get to hear a great many long notes, all thoughtfully finessed and nuanced, though mysteriously left to hang like cobwebs in the ether. In reality, at least as much of the work is being done by the ears as the embouchure, tongue and lungs. There appears to be

---

16 A friend of mine used to dread attending family get-togethers or parties, in case there happened to be a piano skulking in the corner. Though he could play a mean *Waldstein Sonata*, he seemed entirely incapable of summoning a piece he had performed beautifully a year earlier, let alone playing a Christmas carol to order.

an almost meditative value to this, too; it is most definitely mindful. Dizzying flourishes of notes, when at last they come, are blessed with the same degree of colour and resonance as those endless long notes which formed the bulk of the practice session.

When was the last time you sat at the piano and worked on your sound with a similar degree of attentiveness? We may think we are doing this all of the time when, in reality, we hear but we may not actually listen; perhaps we notice tiny fluctuations in tonal evenness, imperfections of balance or asynchronies between the hands; alas we seem often too easily distracted by other more pressing needs. We remember to *crescendo* perhaps, but not to *decrescendo* in equal measure; we might aim to 'bring out the tune', but in doing so overlook the need to tease out the middle or top note in the accompanying chords; we manage to align our pedalling to the changes of harmony perhaps, but take our focus away from the infinitesimal blurring that is playing havoc with the melodic line. All of these things distinguish a good ear from an excellent one, and were we to remember to practise such activities in isolation each time we sit down to do an hour's work, our playing would likely transform beyond recognition.

This leads me to another practical exercise we can get into the habit of doing each day. Voicing, or 'bringing out' notes of perceived importance, is probably the piano's best-kept secret. Bizarrely, a number of advanced players attending my lessons or masterclasses appear to have absolutely no idea how they achieve what they do! In order to create a particular effect on the piano – and, importantly, to be under control of the instrument, we need to be mindfully engaged. We need to be physically relaxed in our playing too, not so intent on pulling off a particular technical 'trick' that we tense up and render the goal impossible. Learning how to relax in our bodies, while keeping all the cogs whirring in our heads, is the Holy Grail in piano playing.

A neat way into voicing, at whatever level one happens to be, is to work with a simple chord until it submits to your most subtly imagined nuances.

1 Begin by playing a right-hand chord repeatedly (any white-note triad will do at first) at a level of *mezzo-forte*, pedal down, slowly and thoughtfully for a minute or two at a time.[17]

2 At each repetition we need to choose a note – top, middle or bottom – and begin to 'work' it so that it slowly eases forward in the mix. As we do so, we pull the finger in question towards us a little more rapidly than its neighbours and hence hear it ping out more clearly. The degree to which this occurs is ultimately a question of the ear's marriage to the finger – this bond will grow over time if you nurture it and really hunger for it.

3 Try the same approach with four-note chords next, then in the left hand, with both hands together, bringing out the bass and top notes simultaneously, in a variety of keys, and so on.[18]

---

17 It is advisable, at least at first, to use fingers 1, 2 and 4, not 1, 3 and 5.

18 The addition of black notes ought not to complicate matters, as long as the fingertips are not permitted to wander too far into the keys. In the majority of 'real-world' scenarios, the nearer to the edge of the keys we are, the more control we have over the sound and individual voicings.

4   Now choose something mellifluous to play, like the opening to your favourite Chopin Nocturne, and apply the same level of discernment in your voicing of the notes in each hand. Care about every note, every relationship between every note and every possible opportunity for pulling out colour and beauty in your sound – just like the diligent, patient flautist.[19]

This little exercise has innumerable potential applications, which will doubtless occur to you as you go about your daily practising – everything from slow hands-separate work to building up the majestic climaxes you are eager to hear yourself produce in Brahms. Try to think of sound, and the cultivation of a perfectly balanced spread of notes between the hands, as an essential component within your gamut of pianistic skills, or as Philip Fowke mentioned in his Foreword, 'the master joiner with his box of tools, sharpened and oiled.' Philip likes to use the phrase 'sound management' to describe this ongoing aspiration for a persuasive piano sound. When the amateur pianist is able to move away from the idea that voicing is some trifling distraction from getting all of those notes under the fingers, the possibilities for personal growth are limitless. Indeed, the often overlooked composer, Franz Reizenstein,[20] considered technique to be merely another word for control, and it is with especial regard to the production of a compelling, communicative piano sound that we can immediately grasp his point.[21]

When we next come to reconsider matters of structure, harmonic schemes and all the other 'heady' accoutrements of piano playing, hopefully an amount of this acute listening will impact too, adding to our music-making more of the fragrance and eloquence it deserves. No amount of analysis or theoretical reduction of a page of music will ever reveal all there is to know about generating excitement or poetry in a musical performance.[22] The music hiding behind the dots calls for our humanity and sense of daredevil, not just our ability to scribble chord symbols under the notes of a Liszt Study, or point out the sonata form in Beethoven's *Tempest*. In truth, we need all of these skills, and the ability to switch our attention from one to the other in an instant, but at the heart of every compelling performance is a wonderfully vivid, cared-for sound, and it is this facet which pianists would do well to prize more highly.

19   When we say we love a particular pianist's sound, I often feel what we really mean is that we adore their manner of connecting up lines on a note-by-note basis, and simultaneously their instinct for revealing 'buried treasure' in the vertical texture. 'Tone versus dynamics' remains a fascinating hot potato (among pianists at least, if not scientists and theorists). If you have a little time on your hands, why not delve into Tobias Matthay's (1858–1945) intriguing, if often controversial viewpoint on 'tone' in piano playing, in particular *The Visible and Invisible in Pianoforte Technique*, 1932, (Oxford, Oxford University Press). Carl Seashore's contemporaneous discussion of tonal gradation, which takes a somewhat polarised stance, makes for an equally fascinating read: Seashore C., 1967: *Psychology of Music* (London, Dover).
20   Franz Reizenstein (1911–1968), an illustrious German-born British composer of much excellent piano music, and professor at London's Royal Academy of Music.
21   My source for this is the composer-pianist (and my professor at the Birmingham Conservatoire, himself a pupil of Reizenstein), Philip Martin.
22   It would seem that the shared concerns of teacher and struggling pianist remain largely ignored in the field of music analysis; very little analysis percolates through in terms which attempt to find practical solutions to recurrent problems.

Towards a more mindful approach

> Practising mindfulness of specific details in music, leads to the development of a larger awareness; you start with focussing on one thing and you gradually develop a more 'panoramic' awareness of the whole piece. This is extremely valuable for a performer, because on stage, we certainly have plenty of panoramic awareness! We become intensely aware of the whole environment we're in. So practising is our opportunity to be mindful of each detail – 'How does this feel in my hand?' 'How does this sound affect me emotionally?' And then, gradually, as we master all of these details, they start coming together and we get this creation.
>
> And when it gets to that point, you have mastered the details enough that you are now ready to go and perform it. The piece has become a part of you, and it flows through you in performance. Then you have enough command of the piece that you can add the huge element of the audience. Up until then, it's just been you and the composer. Now, suddenly, there are all of these people! And this can be shocking when you walk out there. In order to be able to handle that third element you must be fully united with the music, as much as possible. All of this is so challenging that I don't think many people actually get to this point of real command on stage. Madeline Bruser

Among the critical points to grasp in becoming a more mindful pianist is how to manage time efficiently. Resolve to set yourself realistic goals every time you sit down at the piano and aim never to work for more than an hour in a single session; a five-minute rest midway through should be sufficient to rejuvenate you, but do remember to take it. It is also imperative to derive satisfaction from the process of learning and maintaining your standard. Even for a top-flight pianist, the ratio of time spent practising to performing is staggeringly topsy-turvy. (If you were to add up the hours a busy pianist such as Paul Lewis spent on stage last season it may well add up to less than the aggregated time he spent brewing coffee and responding to emails.) Tempting though it may be to allow our thoughts to drift forward to an upcoming performance, too much focus on our 'event horizon' will most assuredly act as a mental energy-sapper. Just as is the case in performing, a key component of effective, purposeful practising is an ability to shut out everything that is not directly relevant to the 'here and now'.

By comparing what you can do now with what you were able to do one hour before, you obtain a more palpable sense of your pace of improvement. Try this as a preliminary exercise:

1 Begin by sitting silently with a piece of music for a few minutes. Place any other volumes of music you are currently learning well out of sight, jettison any frisky cats from the room and put your mobile phone to sleep.

2 Be conscious of your breathing and slowly lock into a sense of attentiveness.

3 Open your notepad and jot down a single objective which you aim to accomplish in the next fifteen minutes – one quarter of the session. Be as unambitious as you like, for initially the task is to achieve your goal and emerge victorious. You are not conquering the world, just fixing a tiny piece of your playing that happens to be temporarily imperfect.

Set yourself up to succeed with bite-sized morsels, and the pathway to more lucrative, fulfilling piano playing will have already begun. For now, just be content to take control and feel good about what you are doing.

I often use a two-pronged approach to introduce the concept of mindful practising. The approach becomes increasingly advantageous once one has achieved a measure of fluency with a piece. First, we make a calm, objective assessment of a short, tricky passage. This will involve continually shifting our attention from the score to our hand(s) and back again; we want to be certain our hand and wrist position are conducive to the work being done. Pianists rarely do enough of this. Though we may notice ungainly movements in other people's playing, such as 'cliff hanging' (wrists collapsing lower than the key bed) or 'tea drinking' (little finger stuck up in the air), we often neglect to self-police. Our hands and fingers are often left to fend for themselves while we stare fixedly at the page. We are also checking to see whether the hand shapes we adopt are optimal for the fingers to function as planned. Though we routinely scribble fingerings into scores, it is of course entirely impractical to sketch in the *hand positions* which will make these achievable; yet actually, this is the source of much of our difficulty. Even relatively advanced pianists frequently move their fingers, hands, arms and elbows far more than is advisable when operating at any speed, rendering the care they have taken over fingering choices virtually redundant. We often fail to see the value in keeping what was at one time termed a 'quiet' hand. In practice, this means positioning the hand and wrist comfortably at the angle needed to allow the fingers to make contact with the notes they will be playing next, as if about to strike a cluster chord. By encouraging the hands to move swiftly and reliably into each new position, the fingers can move with increased dexterity.

The second part of the approach involves quite the reverse tactic. Now that we have taken all sensible precautions with the hand, wrist and fingers at a slow speed in order to minimise extraneous movements, it is time to put this to the test under 'real-world' conditions. This is simply to get a sense of whether the machinery will work just as efficiently when eventually taken up to speed. In summary, first, we work slowly and methodically for several minutes, choreographing every tiny movement – then we immediately go for it at a decent speed to confirm we are potentially on the right track. We can then make small adjustments as necessary, slowly once again, before testing it out at a bolder tempo. Appreciably more time will be spent working at quarter-speed than at full tilt, though this two-pronged approach is key to ensuring all our painstaking spade-work is not in vain.

3 Connecting your mind with your body

Composing yourself

Success begins in the mind. How we start our practice session may well shape the course of events for the next hour or so. Launching headlong into the hardest thing we aim to tackle is not being generous to ourselves, nor is it terribly realistic. We need a moment to gather our composure, organise our thoughts and prepare for what is coming our way. An excellent way of doing this is to shut out the immediate environment for a moment and sit peacefully in your music room. Look around you and enjoy the prospect of having time to yourself; practising is what you have chosen to do, not a chore, so set about your practising with a positive frame of mind. There might be a tempest blowing outside or a televised rugby match going on next door, but no matter, you are going to be making music amid an oasis of calm.[23]

The peace in your head

Begin with some slow, deep breathing. Try not to think of this as an 'exercise' so much as an altered state of being. An amount of mental babble may well be occurring, but not for too long if you are attentive to where you are and what you are poised to do. This is akin to a meditative approach, though not meditation *per se*; nonetheless, it can bring your body and your mind into closer proximity with each other, give yourself a respite from the hustle and bustle of your busy brain and beckon it away from its random freneticism. There is an undeniably broad, very real relationship between our breathing and our heart rate, which is why we can successfully slow the engine to idle if we slow the pace of breathing. Even if we cannot hear ourselves breathe (perhaps we have a meditation track playing in the background) we can still sense it and respond to it.

Count up to six slowly, at least at first, to regulate what you are doing and impose a level of consistency. Try to latch onto the breathing itself and savour the feeling of almost rising up from the seat as you inhale, keeping the same straight-backed posture as you intend to use for your playing in a minute or two's time. I like to imagine my head as a weightless object, perched on the top of my spine like a cricket ball balanced on a stump. Now, as you settle and draw into yourself, slowly switch your attention from your breathing to your right hand; just be aware of its existence – do not actually move it. It feels entirely relaxed, hardly connected to the rest of you at all. The breathing, in and out, continues just as before, but now you are ready to focus on the third finger in

---

23 The 'peace in your head' counts for so much more than the physical silence you may or may not be lucky enough to experience when practising – indeed, conversely there can be times when your environment is dead quiet, but your head is full of noise, in which case it will be even more important to centre your mind and put your body into a conducive, receptive state. Not all noises-off prove to be equally distracting. I find the whirring of a distant lawnmower early on a summer's evening quite beneficial to my concentration when practising, composing or writing.

the same hand; it is just 'there', complicit and attentive, awaiting instructions. Imagine the five fingers to be lightly touching white keys, though strangely enough there is no arm connected to your hand.

Now, as you next draw in your breath, mentally lift the finger to its full extent, as though you were poised to strike a key with considerable force; this upwards motion coincides precisely with the inward breath, and the downward strike will marry to the outward breath. Enjoy the sensation of 'watching' the finger rise, as if operated from above by a system of pulleys and leavers. Perform this slow up-down motion several times, and as you do so, imagine a camera moving slowly around your hand to capture a 360-degree view of your moving finger in time with your breathing.

This simple coupling of the mind to your 'phantom' body will bring you into closer proximity with yourself; at least as importantly, it will tug you ever so gently from distracting thoughts lingering in your mind. From this basic procedure you can begin, on subsequent days, to combine other imagined finger movements – for example, as the third finger of the right hand rises, the fourth finger of the left hand travels down to its key; as the second and fifth fingers of the right hand lift up, the left thumb sinks down to its key – all in slow-motion and precisely in time with the breathing.

You are effectively practising the piano in your head; perhaps you can actually hear the hammers kissing the strings.[24] In your mind's ear, the piano sounds beautifully in tune, perfectly even to the touch, pearly in tone. Notice how full and wholesome each note 'sounds' and 'feels'. Like the cellist, you are living within the sound itself, and like the singer you are controlling the sound not by playing, but by breathing. From here we can move to mentally lifting the wrist of each hand in time with the breathing – upwards/inwards, downwards/outwards – allow the wrist to move from its imagined cup-shaped rest position at the keyboard up to approaching a 'high five' position. Now try combining the imagined finger motions of one hand with the wrist motion in the other. The important thing to bear in mind is the effortless, unhurried ease of what you are doing; the oneness of it all; the immediacy of how it feels. You are now minded and mindful, primed for anything Fauré feels like throwing at you.

When we start a practice session in this way, we introduce the elements of inner sound, inner fingers and inner movements in the simplest, most natural way possible. We become aware of motion at a molecular level and are ready to deal with the complexities of *real* playing, facing an out-of-tune piano or its slightly uneven action without feeling compromised; the piano is what it is, but you almost feel you can make it 'better' simply by caring deeply enough about it. Though I have posited this as a short warm-up, it is also something you can do while watching the news or waiting for the bath to run – in some ways this is even better because you are practising blocking out those things that are not

---

24 'In one study, participants who mentally practised a 5-finger sequence on an imaginary piano for two hours a day had the same neurological changes (and reduction in mistakes) as the participants who physically practised the same passage on an actual piano', Noa Kageyama, www.bulletproofmusician.com

relevant to what you are doing, while simultaneously holding dearly to what matters. You will grow especially fond of your mental instrument and can feel free to open its lid any time you feel like it.

> When I was young I would go to the local library, borrow recordings and scores, and listen whilst following the music; this is something I recommend to all my students. The concentration required to follow a score is a first step towards being able to play music back in your head at will. Like anything else, practice is essential – it doesn't just happen. Find a quiet place, where you will not be interrupted. Take a score and a recording of something short (a Bach invention or Mozart minuet would be good to start with) and listen to the piece a couple of times while following the score. Then, see if you can 'hear' the piece all the way through with the score, but *without* the recording. Don't worry if you don't succeed first time, just try a shorter section. In time, you will be able to do the same with larger works. **John Lenehan**

Channelling your creative focus

Before we can be creative, we need to be in tune with ourselves and at ease with our surroundings. Any tension that has built up during the day will act as a firewall to creative thinking and will quickly burn away any prospect of feeling inspired. Being creative requires the kind of energy we generally reserve for the more special moments in our lives, and piano practice ought to be among these. Ironically, there can be times when our mental resources may have dwindled to a low ebb, yet we find ourselves functioning rather better than usual. It is as though the tiredness (or perhaps adrenaline) is enabling us to tap into reserves we would not normally be aware exist. Clearly we cannot depend on these intermittent quasi-dreamlike states to arise with any predictability. We would be better off building up a bank of more reliable ways by which we can feel centred and ready for doing some creative practising.

The following simple techniques aim to encourage you to savour the sensation of aligning your body, mind and inner ear in pursuit of sharpened focus.

1 Sit upright at the piano and close your eyes. A darkened room should help you to feel calm and not distracted by your surroundings.

2 Place both hands on the keys in random places around the middle register and slowly move your mind to the very tips of your fingers. Relax and try not to carry the weight of your arms in your shoulders; your fingers should feel almost supernaturally connected to the piano; they will not be required to play anything just yet.

3 Breathe slowly and rhythmically as just described, and you will soon feel your heart rate drop a little. Just let yourself 'be' for a while and enjoy the sense of being in touch with the instrument you have grown to love.

4 Prepare to take a long inhalation, and as you do so, physically lift your third finger quite high. Now play a note and try to make it the most poignant,

perfect sound you have ever made. Even without first depressing the pedal you will hear it ring for maybe half a minute or more, depending of course on how fast you depressed the key.[25]

5 As it begins its very slow decay, 'watch' this note (you might imagine being at the top of a very shallow-inclined ski slope, hardly moving at first, just inching your way along), and as this happens, slowly begin to breathe out. The simple act of exhaling, slowly and fully, can be most effective as a means of relaxing. With a little practice, you should be able to coincide each exhalation with the precise striking moment of the note.

6 See if you can do this whole process two or three times back-to-back, on each occasion allowing yourself to inhale a full, deep breath before the next leisurely 'descent'.

The simple act of latching onto your breathing, sounding each long note and turning its audible sensation into something a little more visual, should soon transport you away from your room and make you feel more aware of the life each note lives. Listen with all your concentration and devotion, and be especially aware (as Douglas Finch suggested earlier) of the final seconds of each sound as it thresholds into nothing. It is when the real note has disappeared, but still lives on in your mind's ear, that your focus has peaked.

Once you feel you have channelled your creative focus, and are fully aware of every second each seemingly endless note is sounding, you can begin to connect together two notes, then three or four in closer succession. Count six slow beats for each note and use a different finger randomly, from either hand (they are still all touching various keys), to form a perfect *legato* and *diminuendo*.[26] The idea is to make each note begin at the precise volume the previous one reached at its particular point of decay; it is as if our first skier is smoothly passing a baton to another who has just started moving ahead of him, and this is happening each time a new note is sounded. In a sense, we are attempting to get close to Debussy's apocryphal 'piano without hammers', whereby there is no real beginning to our notes at all, more a 'phaaa' sound than a 'daaa'.

Another invaluable technique involves feeling the cusp of each note as it is repeated; at first, this is best achieved rather slowly and softly.

1 With your eyes closed again, and breathing calmly as before, aim to sense the precise millisecond at which the piano's escape is under way – 'life on the edge', so to speak.

2 Make the up and down movements of the key infinitesimally small – aim for *ppppp* – so that they are barely detectable. The sustain pedal will certainly be needed to make the effect work properly.

---

25 Interestingly, in respect to computer music (and the Midi data which the vast majority of music software packages in some way utilise), what pianists usually think of as 'volume', or 'loudness', is called 'velocity'. It is worth mulling this over when you next sit at the piano: it is the *speed* at which a note travels that will determine how loud it is, not how hard we strike the key.

26 It does not matter which notes you play, just the way they hook up to each other.

As we grow in our sensual awareness of each note as it melds almost imperceptibly into the next, we experience a new hinterland of touch possibilities; at the same time, we are discovering what the instrument itself can manage. When different speeds and dynamics are brought into the equation you will find a 'glancing blow' effect begins to arise quite naturally, whereas when you started the exercise at a very unhurried pace you could really 'feel' the moment of transition occurring, creating a vanishingly small sound. This kind of technical exercise is so fundamental to piano playing, so elemental, and yet most of us have not reacquainted ourselves with the piano in this way since our first joyful exploration of the instrument at the age of six.

Staying in the moment

A negative memory of how things went during yesterday's practice will take some shifting – perhaps you have found yourself taking out your frustration on the piano, or shouting obscenities at a long dead composer. We should begin with exercises designed to stimulate the mind and body, and aim to close off each day with a series of positive musical experiences. Difficulties encountered during practising can build disproportionately into episodes of self-admonishment; the day can become punctuated by a persistent nagging sensation – *I must sort out that sequence in the Schubert! How will I ever master those wretched trills in the Handel?* The deeply-rooted feeling that we are inadequate in some fundamental way is greatly damaging to our state of mind – *I really ought to be able to play that simple prelude, what on earth's wrong with me?* These self-doubts linger and multiply, polluting our day long after the practising has ended. This affects how kind we are to the cat, but it may also harm our perilously fragile psychological balance to a point where we may avoid practising altogether. Being troubled by a fleeting sense of inadequacy is one thing, but in extreme circumstances we become subsumed by entrenched feelings of incapacity and insecurity.

Are you an inveterate planner? I am. There is nothing intrinsically wrong with the act of thinking ahead to the next event in our musical lives, except that these thoughts can act as a drain on our sense of the present moment. For this reason, always do your planning away from the piano. An ability to live in the moment implies a certain capability to switch off our concerns or excitement about what lies ahead. If we become too far-sighted in our pianistic ambitions, we will have little time or mental energy left for dealing with the 'here and now'. The result is that instead of enjoying our practising, and feeling content with slowly getting to grips with the immediate task we have set ourselves, we become diverted by some tangential longer-term objective, which in any case cannot happen unless we succeed in our current venture.

Part 2

Practising

4 Fingers at the ready

Decisive digits

Piano playing is a fine motor skill. As with all such skills, we need to be continually revisiting our technique, reconsidering it and refining it.[27] Then there is the business of stamina, both physical and mental. As Jascha Heifetz famously quipped, 'If I don't practise one day, I know it; two days, the critics know it; three days, the public knows it'.[28] One of the drawbacks in compartmentalising our playing into 'technique', 'aural', 'interpretation' etc., which for entirely practical reasons we all tend to do, is that we do not always manage to connect it all up into something coherent. We need to be zoned into what we are doing, really thinking about each movement (and *non*-movement) of every finger, noticing whether one wrist is higher than the other, and so on.

Table-tapping and dummy keyboard practice

Here is a little practice scenario for you to try as a 'loosener'.[29]

1 Before you have actually played a single note on the piano, close the lid, place the score on the stand and 'ghost' a passage of music that is troubling you by tapping incisively onto the wood. Try to position your fingers as they will be on the keyboard by imagining the precise spacing of the notes lying directly under the lid.

2 If you are able to hear the music moving along in your mind's ear, so much the better, and try singing out loud as you play.

3 After each ghosting, pause, breathe a few times and consider what just took place; after all, practising without a concrete idea of what you are attempting to fix is a contradiction in terms.

4 Having ghosted through the section a handful of times, see if you can detect any recurrent shortcomings. This is achieved by feel as much as by the sound of your fingers striking the lid, so listen intently, harness your sensory awareness and respond decisively. If your ghosting is uneven, your real playing will be, too.

5 Glance down from time to time to monitor how your hands are shaped, and aim to eradicate any ungainly, jerky movements. At all times remain calm in

---

27 The Canadian pianist, Glenn Gould (1932–1982), was taught by Alberto Guerrero at the Toronto Conservatory. Guerrero taught Gould a technique called 'finger tapping' (Guerrero had apparently encountered something similar at a Chinese circus, where a young boy was rehearsing a dance). If I recall correctly, the technique involved using the finger of one hand to 'tap' the fingertip on the other hand (which would be placed at rest over a key, in a relaxed state); the key would strike its note and then return, demonstrating the minimum force actually required to press down that key. Why not try this yourself?

28 Jascha Heifetz (1901–1987), the Russian violin supremo whose performing career spanned some 65 years.

29 You could of course alternate this with the exercises already given.

your head and relaxed in your wrists and fingers. Tension is most certainly the pianist's *bête noire* – as self-defeating as driving with one foot on the accelerator and the other on the brake.

This exercise will have taken you perhaps five minutes, and though it may seem a little austere as a method of waking up your mind and fingers, it is arguably going to be the most useful part of your session.[30] When, finally, you prepare to play the passage for real, the slate is still clean, yet you have already begun to improve. You should find yourself unusually focussed and aware of what is happening; each movement of the fingers will feel suppler, while your muscular memory should seem noticeably more responsive. The sound you make will be vivid, more alive and controlled. Congratulations, you have just given yourself a piano lesson.[31]

Scales revisited

Scales and studies need not be the bugbear they frequently are allowed to become. A little ingenuity can transform tedious repetition into pleasantly mindful activities. There surely cannot be a teacher in the land who is unaware that scales and arpeggios permeate 'real' pieces at every turn. A great many of Scarlatti's 555 sonatas are riddled with them, let alone the raft of meatier sonatas that emerged in the hundred years following. But simply knowing how important scales are will not make us excited about practising them. We lack the courage of our convictions in this area, and mostly allow exam boards to put a veto on our resourcefulness. Exam boards do not 'own' scales; we must be brave enough to continue on from where exam boards, in their wisdom, choose to stop. We are not in the business of pumping iron, but refining the pathways to a fundamental skill-set. The moment scales become mindless, they are rendered valueless.

A point worth reinforcing is that practising scales and arpeggios can unwittingly become self-serving – they may slowly improve, but in a vacuum, strangely cut off from the rest of our playing. The subtle variants of scales, which crop up naturally in piano pieces, renders them just that little bit aloof from the daily grind of formal scale practising; for some, this is all the excuse that is needed to push them to one side.

Let us briefly remind ourselves what we get from rehearsing scales and arpeggios: key/pattern awareness, nimbleness, coordination/synchronisation, independence of fingers, relaxed wrists, confident coverage of the keyboard, equality and balance of hands. There are more besides these 'machine'-based attributes, but these are surely sufficient to justify the existence of scales and arpeggios, even if there had never been a piece composed that required them.

---

30 If you are practising on an electric piano, you may now wish to ensure the volume is turned right down and proceed to play as if on a dummy keyboard.

31 Should you find yourself with a little spare cash, you might consider purchasing (or hiring) a 'real' dummy keyboard; some brands sell two models: 25 keys and 85 keys. They are surprisingly good to work with, and some have adjustable key depths (and even black keys adjustable to different heights).

Instead of looking to Clementi for evidence that we need scales, how about looking at Ravel? Here we are sometimes required to play two 'scales' at the same time, albeit in snippets or interrupted with pattern-breakers. A glance at many of John McLeod's more virtuosic piano pieces should be sufficient to demonstrate how important it is to be able to 'split' the mind into two or more parts when tackling certain passages.[32] These are real-world scenarios that composers have designed in order to achieve a rather special effect, so why not evolve an approach which makes play of these frankly more interesting figurations?

For many years I have threaded scales and arpeggios into my teaching surreptitiously, for fear of the palpable groan which may result. But in other scenarios a more direct, candid approach usually works best, especially at piano summer schools, where there is a need to broaden the experience and keep things more light-hearted, perhaps for a small mixed-ability group. I tripped over the following exercises quite by accident, but they have stood me in good stead. I am quite positive you will never find any of these on an examination board's list of 'prepared tests', but they are no less worthy for that.

Arpscalpaggios

My philosophy is to transmogrify the humble scale into a sort of 'extended technique'. Try playing two scales (or two arpeggios) at once, for example C major in the right hand and F♯ major in the left; *staccato* in one hand, *legato* in the other; *piano* and *forte* simultaneously; triplets in the left hand and duplets in the right; with the hands two, three or even four octaves apart – these are all excellent brainteasers as well as finger-busters. Five minutes of these spliced into your daily practising will certainly not be time wasted. The aim is not to evolve a bank of party tricks with which to impress your fellow pianists (though they probably will), but to engage the mind more actively and gainfully. If you are a lapsed scale-player, or a teacher with pupils whose first reaction is to slump at the very mention of them, why not weave these hybridised exercises (I call them 'arpscalpaggios') into the playing and savour the transformation that occurs? Below are a few written-out variants for you to be going on with. Doubtless, you will quickly come up with your own bespoke versions.

Arpscalpaggios example 1

---

32 John McLeod CBE, Scottish composer born in 1934, with whom I have been fortunate enough to collaborate on a number of occasions. McLeod's piano music – five sonatas, a concerto, and much more besides – invites careful consideration by the contemporary player interested in music which actually 'works', from a practical as well as musical perspective.

Arpscalpaggios example 2

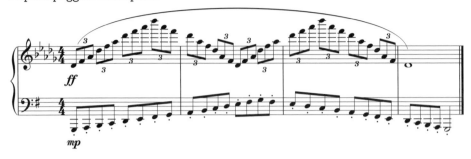

Arpscalpaggios example 3

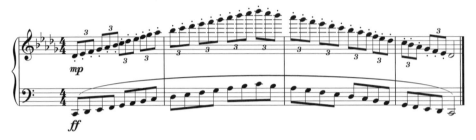

'**Volume fader**' Here you are required to alter the volume in either hand markedly up and down at someone else's instruction. Start with both hands at *mezzo forte*, and obey your friend as s/he moves one hand or the other up or down from a resting position of both hands equidistant from the floor, starting about waist height. Again, this encourages independence of brain patterning, but at the same time brings welcome relevancy to the process of practising repetitive movements.

Volume Fader

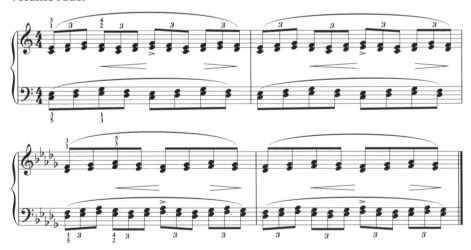

'**Dramatic chromatics**' My favourite home-grown exercise cultivates melody voicing while simultaneously playing something altogether different in the same hand. It is surely worth reflecting upon a point made earlier in the book, namely that when we think we are practising a finger- or wrist-based activity we are essentially practising a brain activity; for all our talk of kinaesthetic memory, the fingers are merely compliant servants, they do not have minds of their own.

Dramatic chromatics

For many players, creating exercises out of tricky passages in pieces – i.e. context-based – achieves everything scales and studies set out to do. I do not entirely agree with this; even if we do not feel our fingers need a regular workout, we surely accept that our brains do. For one thing, scales and arpeggios force us to practise the turnaround at the top (and/or bottom), which in my experience as an examiner is where much of the difficulty in piano playing is to be found. In short, hardly any activity we pianists routinely practice will prove more profitable than taking a more mindful approach to our scales and arpeggios.

Schumann once reflected that 'one should always play as if in the company of a master'. If your mind begins to drift when you are playing them, you need to ratchet up the difficulty level a notch or two, for example by checking your progress against a metronome or coming up with ever more fiendishly fun combinations. I was once able to get a rather advanced teenager to do all of these things while reciting his seven times table – a wilfully bizarre scenario perhaps, but so much more potentially rewarding than the myriad multi-tasking games you can download onto your iPad to while away a rainy evening.

5 Playing to your strengths

Get your ducks in a row

In conversation with a physical education teacher recently, I learned that regular gym-goers commonly find the middle of their workout the least pleasurable part of the overall experience – they look forward to training, and indeed relish the satisfaction of knowing they have been to the gym, but are generally less enamoured by the sweaty bit in the middle when all the graft is being done. I cannot help wondering if there is an underlying parallel with piano practice. We are all familiar with the sensation of having allowed our practising to slip, and how subsequently overcoming the inertia can take considerable willpower, but once we are in some kind of routine we usually slip easily into our preferred way of working and soon find ourselves hard at it.

> Allocate a conducive time of day to work, taking five minutes to clear your mind beforehand. Relax your upper body particularly. When sitting at the piano, allow your arms to fall freely by your side, feeling heavy and totally free of tension. As you put your hands on the keys, ensure a comfortable, flexible hand position, with loose wrists, relaxed arms and unrestricted elbows. A few warm-up exercises, played very slowly, with fingers key-bedding, can be helpful physically and can also encourage complete focus. Sight-reading sets the scene for concentrated work; reading is demanding, and by utilizing this element at the beginning of a practice session, you will sharpen your reflexes and activate the thought process. You're now ready to start. Technical exercises, or scales and arpeggios, may be a beneficial vehicle for every practice regime before tackling intended repertoire. Always take regular breaks and aim to keep a positive outlook. Melanie Spanswick

It is undoubtedly a good idea to keep a checklist, or perhaps to devise some other means of summing up your piano practice workload on a daily, weekly or even monthly basis. In addition to this, many people scrupulously keep a notebook which they take with them to piano lessons so that they can jot down ideas and strategies. Notebooks are often replete with questions: some will have been answered by the teacher, some remain eternally rhetorical. The more diligent among us might pester our teachers to notate a particular exercise, for example to build better 4th finger independence, or we may even photograph our teacher's hand as it accomplishes a specific skill. Increasingly, especially for consultation lessons, I find people asking permission to record the entire lesson for their own personal use. Although this process necessarily involves extra work during the lesson (and can, if taken to an extreme, become a rod for our back), it is clearly the case that we need touch-points to assist with cross-referencing all the ideas that our musical lives tend to fling in our direction. I am still learning from throwaway comments directed at me from masterclasses and piano lessons dating back several decades, though I admit to having always been quite slack when it comes to taking notes.

The question of payback – the degree to which all this is actually helping us – can only be answered by the person who has expended the effort. Some people who have attended my summer schools or other masterclass-style events seem to be scribbling copious notes throughout, while others just sit back and drink it all in. What happens after the session is anyone's guess – I suspect often the notes simply mount up randomly and never see the light of day again. But perhaps this does not matter. Arguably it is the act of *making* the notes that defines their true value.

Mind maps

Mind maps are a method of ordering and expressing our thoughts dreamed up by Tony Buzan of Mensa nearly half a century ago.[33] Buzan's approach has myriad possible applications in our daily lives, indeed the Internet is teeming with examples of impressive looking mind maps created by avid exponents. Central to the approach is that we tend to be better able to assimilate thoughts when expressed graphically, often with heavy use of colour and images, rather than in 'boring' shopping-list form.[34] They are called 'maps' for the obvious reason that they partly resemble a route map – lines, words, pictorial references – all of which explode out from the middle of the page into the various strands.

Although the creator of a mind map will also generally be the person who refers to it, time and again, arguably its chief advantage over other more conventional approaches is the process itself. Ever heard of the 'Ten Times Rule'? It works according to the premise that we will tend to remember something if we write it (see it, or play it) ten times. We embed it into our brain so that it becomes almost a part of who we are.

We can see from both these models that there may be a solution to keeping track of all the precious, randomly accumulated thoughts that occur to us, and locking them into our consciousness once and for all. If your brain works best by building up spatial elements and joining them together, mind maps may well be the way forward. The mind map given on page 46 demonstrates their potential for us as mindful pianists. It illustrates a week's piano practice at a glance. You may prefer to sketch out a mind map *after* you have done your practising to reflect on what was actually accomplished, rather than as a means of keeping you on track at the time. As with any new concept, you will need practice at coming up with effective incarnations of your own, but remember that these never need to be seen by anyone else, and you might soon be rattling them off on the back of an envelope as you sit in the dentist's waiting room.

33 www.mensa.org.uk
34 Family trees bear a striking resemblance to mind maps.

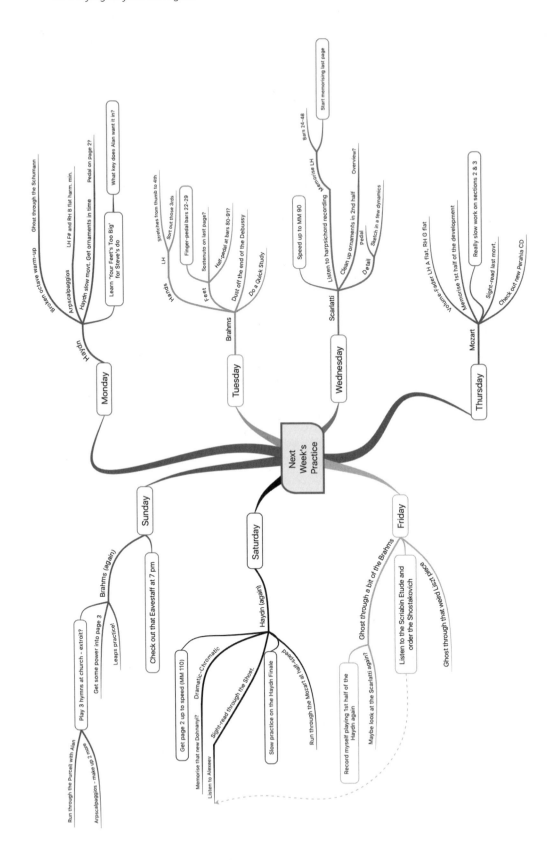

You might also wish to consider the potential for using a mind map to orientate you while performing. A mental mind map can serve as a prompt to keep your overview intact, perhaps to nudge you in matters of memorisation, or to reassure you about the running order for your concert programme.[35] Improvisers especially can gain a great deal from having a safety net, or even by laying out plausible harmonic 'directions' in which to head. All of these ideas are merely starting points of course, things to mull over as you develop agility and freedom with your mind maps; doubtless, you will come up with many adaptations of your own.

Keeping repertoire in perspective

Good repertoire choice is crucial to both progression and motivation, yet with the wealth of inspiring piano music we have at our beck and call, it is very easy to let our heart decide what to play next. This can lead to the 'candyfloss' approach to choice – what's immediately appealing is occasionally unrewarding and often not good for our musical nourishment.

Allow yourself the occasional indulgence, but balance your choice of repertoire across the broadest range of styles and periods; they are all tributaries to a healthy musical river. Playing solely Romantic repertoire is like a high-jumper only training his jumping leg; it works for a while, but then he realises there are limits to the height he can aspire to. Challenge yourself to consider repertoire that has stood the test of time on the concert platform, but that you might not immediately warm to, aiming to understand what has given it its enduring appeal; learning the language of an unfamiliar composer can lead to a lifelong love affair.

Avoid repertoire where the personal challenges are predominantly playing the notes themselves. Instead, choose pieces where your aspiration is to play with the level of sophistication, tonal colour and fluency of your favourite pianist; playing a simple piece exquisitely is one of the hardest things a professional pianist has to do. Finally, sight-read, sight-read and *sight-read* through music, even music you 'think' you are familiar with. There are gems out there from mainstream composers still relatively undiscovered. Don't wait for them to appear in an exam syllabus, put on your explorer's hat and enter into the wonderful, cavernous library that is our pianistic inheritance. **Anthony Williams**

Your hand size and stretch will, in all probability, appear to equip you more readily to certain styles or composers; moreover, being able to form an opinion quickly regarding what you do best is all part of becoming more mindful. We are each of us born with certain attributes, even those which others may regard as failings. If we are fortunate enough to be shown how to channel our energies

---

35 I recall doing something akin to this when memorising the key-scheme in Chopin's 24 Preludes, to rather good effect.

in the most lucrative directions, capitalising on our lean fingers for playing Debussy perhaps, or our muscularity for tackling Scriabin, we can achieve wonderfully satisfying piano playing.

While finding the right piece for you has to be one of the most joyful eureka moments for any pianist, choosing inappropriate repertoire is perhaps the single most debilitating aspect of piano playing over which we have influence. This criticism is especially, though by no means exclusively, pitched at adult learners, particularly those who are self-taught. Doggedly fixing on a piece that is patently too difficult is a little like insisting on buying the wrong-sized shoes simply because you love the style – you hobble about like a giraffe on stilts, ignoring the consternation shown in the faces of passers-by. We need to accept and celebrate the peculiarities of our physical stature and make these work for us: short people do not generally make expert basketball players, and tall people are rarely derby-winning jockeys – certainly, we can push the boundaries and enjoy tussling courageously with music that is a notch or two too difficult, but ultimately we are deluding ourselves if we insist upon tackling repertoire which does not match our current physique and artistic capacities.

I sometimes hear from diploma candidates that they have chosen a piece because they felt it might be 'good for them' in some way (like cod liver oil, presumably), which is not always a very convincing argument. Alternatively, the teacher may have picked the piece, possibly because they know it well and can play it themselves, or because it fits tidily into a realm of piano playing they feel comfortable with; again, this is not necessarily a robust way forward since it overlooks the pupil's own highly specific skill-set and physicality. The piano repertoire is so vast that there is rarely any need to be spending time learning music that isn't able to touch our hearts and at the same time fit well under our fingers. Successful pianists tend to be those whose self-awareness is acute – they have weighed up their options sensibly, preferably with the aid of a strong, liberally-minded teacher.[36] Arguably, the repertoire we wisely chose to put to one side will turn out to be more impactful than the music we opt to learn.

---

36 Moreover, it is important to be able to resist the dangerous parallel between tackling difficult pieces and going for a workout in the gymnasium, forever pushing the limits of one's strength and endurance regardless of the collateral damage being inflicted on one's body and psyche.

6 What pianists do

Performance: Composition in reverse

It might be useful to imagine a musical score as a paper-trail of clues leading back to the music's initial construction. A composer's crossings-out and/ or subsequent revisions to a musical work can provide interesting evidence regarding the order in which important ideas were dreamed up. Not unlike an architect's drawings, these clues can remain in place centuries after a piece was composed. As a result, in certain works, such as Rachmaninov's Second Sonata, pianists are free to choose which version they prefer to play from.[37] We still need to know the basic 'rules' of construction of course. While we do not all necessarily pick up on the same clues during our study of a piano score, it is these things which will implant themselves most deeply into our understanding during the learning process.[38] They function rather like bookmarks, flagging up pivotal moments in the music when something important is about to take place, such as a false recapitulation in a Beethoven sonata or an unannounced modulation in a tango by Piazzolla.

I recently gave the première of a six-movement piano concerto in which repeated arpeggio-type figurations peppered the score, page after page.[39] Had I not consciously counted '19 of these...and now 12 of those' I would have been well and truly scuppered, especially since many of the patterns were similar but not identical. For this reason, I find myself slightly at variance with one of the recurring themes in Barry Green's ground-breaking book, *The Inner Game of Music*,[40] in which musicians are encouraged to cleanse themselves of thoughts relating to the construction of a piece during the act of performing.[41] It goes without saying that when we are in the hot-seat we need to be free of self-doubt and not held back by the fear of failure, but I contend there is a world of difference between confidence-draining gremlins and carefully lodged memory triggers.

I have always instinctively felt that, to some extent, performing amounts to composition in reverse.[42] As pianists, an important ongoing challenge therefore is to dare to fathom the thought process which led to the creation of the music. This necessarily involves a significant amount of speculation,

---

37 In performing Rachmaninov's Sonata No.2 in B flat minor Op.36, pianists may either choose the original version of 1913, lasting 25 mins, or the revised version of 1931, which effectively shaves off about one quarter (or, indeed, Vladimir Horowitz's own authorised version of 1940, which falls roughly mid-way between the two).

38 Some pianists appear convinced a score by, say, Mozart or Chopin, tells us everything we could possibly need to know. On balance, the accrued experience of playing other pieces by these composers may well be what gives them the confidence to interpret decisively.

39 Colin Decio's Concerto 'In Memoriam John Ogdon', world première with the GSO at Cheltenham Town Hall, 2015.

40 Green, B. and Gallwey, W.T., 1986: *The Inner Game of Music* (London, Pan).

41 I do however wholeheartedly concur with another important tenet of the book, which is that the devil on your shoulder must be silenced if a performance is to emerge unencumbered.

42 Heinrich Schenker (1868–1935) reflected that his main reason for learning to compose was to gain the tools needed to analyse and theorise.

though a modicum of structural understanding and a natural resonance with the composer's strategies can all help. From here we may begin to allow our spontaneous intellect a certain amount of considered involvement; if we are lucky, the result will be something memorably beautiful, which the composer might have enjoyed hearing.

> When learning a new piece, we need to start by establishing our own instinctive and very natural relationship with the work. Our intuitive understanding can then be deepened and enhanced by studying the score in all its detail, and by analysing the technique (fingering, movements, gestures and touch) required to realise the composer's intentions as fully as possible. This mental preparation should ideally be done as early as possible in the learning process to allow time for our conscious thoughts and movements to settle and become internalised. As we approach a performance, however, we need to put aside all analytical or critical thought, reignite our imagination and again fully immerse ourselves in the intangible qualities of the music. In this way, instinct and understanding work together to communicate the music very directly in all its richness. **Penelope Roskell**

Expression

What exactly is expression, anyway? Expression, and indeed expressiveness, turns out to be a good deal harder to pin down than one might suppose.[43] When we perform, are we just going through some convoluted box-ticking exercise – dutifully obeying the *accelerando* in bar 46 and paying lip-service to the *piano* in bar 91?[44] Roy Howat makes a good case for not seeing expression as a bolt-on: '"Put some expression into it!" is still a ubiquitous cry even at conservatoires, notwithstanding the contradiction in terms.'[45] Even if this was a worthy objective, the notion of achieving 'fidelity' when reading from a score presupposes a level of objectivity and consistency among pianists which in all probability can never exist.[46] In truth, dynamics, articulation and tempo remain to a significant extent subjective when it comes to their realisation in performance, no matter how prescriptive a composer may *appear* to have been, or how diligent a pianist sets out to be.

The mindful pianist ought to be at least partly intrigued by the conundrum of what is 'expressive' versus what is 'structural' in the music we have chosen to play, for it is on this razor's edge that all of our powers of communication must come alive. Actually, this is the kind of debate which has been floating

43 The question of whether a dynamic marking, *rallentando*, or trill may be seen as functioning structurally or expressively, is central to discussions in prominent contemporary writers, such as Eric Clarke and John Rink.
44 What ultimately matters in respect to building a piano performance, are those aspects of the score which do *not* lend themselves readily to identification or quantification – the music 'behind' the notation, not the notation itself.
45 Howat R., 1995: *What do we perform?*, in 'The Practice of Performance: Studies in Musical Interpretation', Rink J., Ed (Cambridge, CUP), p.3.
46 One of the many problems with the notion of fidelity, or indeed authenticity, is the spurious assumption that 'other' performances are not authentic.

in the ether for quite some time now. In decades (and indeed centuries) past, music analysis concerned itself principally with what the score seemed willing to offer up to the inquisitive onlooker, as distinct from what *performers* might feel inclined to contribute.[47] The unquestioned presumption was that the score, once 'deciphered', was the font of all knowledge; in other words, music analysis equals *score* analysis.

This somewhat narrow, marginalising view of what the pianist does and does not do, led to a welcome paradigm shift in approach during the 1980s: 'Performance Analysis'. At the vanguard of this movement were writers from across the pond, united in their zeal to understand how performers achieve the seemingly impossible – to turn an inanimate score into a majestic, stirring musical experience.[48] To use the modern vernacular, this could be described as the 'value added' by the performer. This is not some trifling philosophical or semantic question, but one which strikes at the very heart of what piano performance is actually all about. Jonathan Dunsby raised the possibility of 'ecstatic music', by which he appears to be distinguishing the immediate impact of music for an audience from the considerably more constructivist approach to grappling with the details necessarily taken by the pianist.[49] But there are surely other entirely plausible ways of unpacking the problem of expression in piano playing awaiting discovery, and like it or not the problem rears its head every time we inch towards the keyboard nursing some vague idea about how a piece could go.

Of one thing pianists can perhaps feel more confident: expressiveness is the opposite of predictability. Arturo Michelangeli's apparent obsession with arpeggiating chords can, at times, lead us to feel we know what he is going to do next; surely we all need to examine ourselves from time to time to ensure we are not falling into a similar trap.[50] The deliberate delaying of a melody note, or 'asynchrony', is another 'old chestnut' that young pianists seem inclined to latch onto the minute they have enjoyed hearing it in someone else's playing.

47 Wallace Berry (1928–1991) sought to show that composers from all time periods emphasise expressive/structural high points using conventional methods, and that these can be elucidated from the score alone. Berry viewed the score as the embodiment of discrete yet interconnected elements, which combine to bring about the composer's predetermined goal(s). He focused on music's capacity to stimulate a sense of direction towards and away from these goals, its ebb and flow of intensity. His work might be understood as helping to consolidate the canonical rules of Western art music.

48 Berry's impact upon the ever-broadening sphere of analysis is manifest in the diverse empirical methods adopted by John Rink, Eric Clarke, Roy Howat, Neil Todd, Manfred Clynes, John Sloboda and others. Taken as a whole, their research would, however, appear to challenge Berry in at least one important respect: the emphasis they place on the function of the *performer* as an active protagonist in bringing the inanimate score to life. While Berry chose to focus on the mechanics of the score in isolation, Rink *et al* have concentrated on evaluating the product itself, that is, the music as a compelling artistic experience. I urge all mindful pianists to invest in a copy of two books: Rink, J. (Ed.), 1995: *The Practice of Performance: studies in musical interpretation* (Cambridge, CUP); also, Cook, N., 1999: *A Guide to Musical Analysis* (Oxford, OUP).

49 Dunsby, J., 1995: *Performing Music: Shared Concerns* (Oxford, OUP). In Anthony Gritten's (University of East Anglia) expedient summary of Dunsby's book, we learn how the author 'attempts to encapsulate his views on the relationship between making music and thinking, by exposing the fundamental role that chance plays in musical performance and by weighing this against the fact that we are nevertheless constrained to "pattern" the world.' (http://escom.org).

50 Arturo Benedetti Michelangeli (1920–1995), Italian pianist of extraordinary gifts, whom Paderewski considered to be magnificent and about whom Cortot declared 'here is a new Liszt'. My point regarding the pianist's preoccupation with arpeggiation is slightly tongue-in-cheek; indeed, in fairness, Michelangeli needs to be understood as a corollary of his day. I particularly love Michelangeli's sound – he achieves a painful, yearning effect, especially in slow Romantic music.

One could even venture to suggest that vibrato in string players leans in the direction of inexpressiveness when it is applied with one medium-sized brush; and then of course there is the singer who feels unable to resist swooping up to every rising note, regardless of whether she is singing *A Nightingale Sang in Berkeley Square* or Purcell's sublime *Music for a While*. Though I suspect many of us unwittingly contribute to the boiling pot of hackneyed expressive 'tricks', ultimately these things cannot really be thought of as serving the music, only the musician, for they function almost like a nervous tick. Our subconscious or perhaps self-conscious patterns of behaviour end up defining us; at the same time, we make it harder for successive generations of players to be truly open-minded. With every uncensored overindulgence, it is as if pianists distance themselves a molecule further away from the composer, who from the annals of time is relying upon our mindfulness and resourcefulness to 'create' on his or her behalf. At regular points in the learning of a new piece we need to be revisiting this miniature debate, not in the misguided hope of finding a conclusive 'solution', but in pursuit of a satisfying compromise between the composer's markings and our own intuitive ideas. When we manage this effectively in performance, it should feel almost as though we composed the piece ourselves.

Transcending our egos

Even if we can never be entirely sure what expression is, most of us take it for granted that performing piano music is all *about* expression – expression of the composer and of ourselves, channelled through the medium of our instrument. After all, this is why we sometimes interchange the word technique for 'facility' – for the technique is meant to be there to facilitate something greater than itself. But we are also familiar with the player who prizes technique over what is being expressed; the tail that wags the dog, as it were. Where this happens, technique becomes a badge of honour; like a new tattoo it is 'in our face', daring us not to notice it. Though all instruments have exponents who fall foul of this, the piano, in my opinion, is in a league of its own. I dare say the showman is somewhere in all of us; a genie dressed like Liberace living in the bottle, waiting for its big moment to come. But, at its extreme, one can actually feel aggressed by a pianist's technique, because instead of it being put to valuable musical purpose, it is simply there to serve itself: *look at me*.[51] Music will always be the loser when the ego transcends what is expressed, or when the urge to dazzle with one's fingers proves more irresistible than the impulse to communicate an uncomplicated musical thought.[52]

A question continually worth asking ourselves, especially as we prepare to stride up on the spot-lit stage and take our applause, is: shall I play this as

---

51 Some tennis players possess a fantastic serve or a spectacular drop-shot; some are touch players and some are powerhouses; I guess we can all think of pianists around us who fit somewhere in this analogy.

52 On the other hand, it is most certainly good to look pleased with yourself when you have performed well in front of others – take your applause graciously and cherish it; you have earned it.

fast as I know I can, or as fast as the music requires? Until we begin to trouble ourselves with this type of question, we cannot claim to be worthy 'custodians' of musical expression. If there is an equivalent of *yin yang* among composers, perhaps it is Liszt and Satie (or Bartók and Couperin, Mompou and Boulez?); they all deserve our utmost sensitivity, else their voices will not be heard above our deafening egos.

Making interpretive decisions

The final arbiter of what works in piano performance comes down to our own entirely subjective (and ultimately ephemeral) estimation of good taste. Imagine a hypothetical world in which we are united in one opinion regarding the boundary that separates good taste from crude posturing – surely there would be no need for more than one concert pianist to exist? Mercifully, we live in a world where diverse opinions count, where fuzzy edges divide one lucid performance from another, and in which we are encouraged to change our minds in light of new experiences and enlightenments. After all, one man's painfully slow Beethoven performance is another's supreme eloquence. The hundreds of recorded performances of works such as Satie's eternally popular *Gymnopédies* demonstrate unequivocally that there is still wriggle-room for each pianist to be expressive. It is worth considering my following 'thought for the day'. Even Mozart had to *interpret* Mozart; not unlike the rest of us, no two performances by him would have been identical.

Perhaps the worst sin we can commit as performers is to hedge our bets. Whereas score analysts might strategically leave open certain questions, undecided as to where, for example, the recapitulation occurs in a Romantic piano sonata, the performer is obliged to pin his/her colours to the mast on a bar-by-bar basis. The act of performance is of course temporal – it unfolds in real time – which is quite the reverse of a painting, fixed by brackets to a wall, unchanging and unaffected by time and tide.[53] In music performance however, the pianist's individuality must mediate between the composer's conception and the needs of the contemporary listener, rendering every performance a vibrantly new, one-off experience for the audience, which could hardly contrast more with what a visitor gains from a trip to an art gallery.[54] For all these reasons it becomes necessary for performers to orate, to communicate and to take risks.[55]

53 Once the picture is complete, arguably the painter's work is done – she can sit at home with a pot of coffee and weigh up options for the next project – and although a curator may still exert a degree of opinion regarding the relative positioning of the pictures within a gallery, lighting etc., in the final count it is the *viewer* who does all of the interpreting.
54 The issue of 'receptivity' among listeners and viewers, i.e. how we all perceive art forms differently, is of course an entirely different question, for which there is insufficient space to explore within these pages.
55 In later life, Arthur Rubinstein reflected 'At every concert I leave a lot to the moment. I must have the unexpected, the unforeseen. I want to risk, to dare.' (UALR Public Radio interview, retrieved 2012.) On the other hand, we would do well to remember that pianists are not adrenaline-junkies – our impulse to preserve dignity in public performance should always be greater than the allure of a fleeting moment's glory. For example, taking a capricious piece at an impossibly slick pace – or, conversely, 'milking' every conceivable poetic invitation in a slow Romantic work – both stray beyond a measured response to the musical possibilities.

> The process of learning a new work, to me, is like an allegory to life;
> one is faced with a multitude of decisions, some more pertinent than
> others. And, not unlike life, there will be many compromises to be
> made along the way, for it takes a lifetime of experience to know how to
> accommodate decisions in the least obtrusive way. **Brian Ellsbury**

Think about what a concert pianist has to do when preparing for a
performance, and how the colossal number of decisions necessarily impact
on the final interpretation. A neat way of gauging this can be achieved using a
modern digital keyboard. A performance given on a high-quality digital piano
can be saved as a performance Midi file, which can then be digitally converted
into a score. Assuming a note perfect rendition, this score would appear as
different from an urtext edition as one could possibly countenance! While
computer-generated scores almost invariably *sound* pretty ghastly, computer-
recorded 'live' performances often *look* far worse; this serves to demonstrate
the limitations of any score, however immaculately conceived, even before we
come to attempt a meaningful performance.

The vital missing link in any piano score will always be the pianist. But, rather
importantly, this is not because the score awaits *replication*. Indeed, thankfully,
pianists have little inclination – and even less practical capability – for precise
replication. We can never be entirely faithful to a score. Even if we could, we
would doubtless abhor what we hear, for it would not amount to a performance
at all. Any attempt to disentangle the performer's note-by-note decisions from
the details which populate the score is about as realistic as reconstructing
carrots out of vegetable soup.

Keeping sight of the bigger picture

Surely one of the hardest things to pull off in performance is a coherent
overview. Linked inextricably with this is knowing 'when to stop'– we
tweak and titivate, fiddle and finesse all the while, perhaps unknowingly
wringing the very life force out of our original conception. The reason we
feel compelled to do so would appear to be this: when learning a piece, we
dutifully acknowledge as many of the details as we can, but paradoxically
the more successful we are in achieving this, the less compelling the bigger
picture will tend to be. By definition, performers cannot prioritise *everything* –
not every detail can be treated as reverentially as its neighbours; if it were, the
end result would be preposterous. Somewhere along the line, pianists need
to exercise discrimination and decide which details to promote, which to
sublimate – and frankly, which to ignore. This is all a part of being a decisive,
purposeful musician. Realising when we have 'got there' remains one of
our greatest challenges, and it would seem one which only becomes more
troublesome as we advance in our playing and the complexities accumulate.
The secret to achieving an incisive musical overview is often hiding in plain
sight – it calls for an ability to 'zoom out' from all the details and take a crow's
nest view.

As our confidence in our interpretation of a particular passage within a piece grows, we may begin to notice how it might best fit within the music's grander framework – suddenly, a broader strategy seems not just possible but entirely desirable. Then we suddenly realise that an important moment among many other important moments is screaming out for attention later on in the music; hence it now occurs to us that its earlier incarnation may not be so important after all. In this scenario, our thoughts regarding *rubato*, or perhaps dynamics, may call for a more restrained approach in order to point up the perceived moment of heightened intensity. Importantly, only some of the signals which could point to this decision may actually be present in the score; the rest is waiting inside the pianist.[56] Indeed, spotting how each section knits together is a crucial part in the process of evolving a feasible overview for our performance; we must be continually on the lookout for the clues that can help us to form a memorable account.[57] There is a paradox here: we will always want to enjoy the moment, yet excessive spotlighting will blind us to what else we might have noticed.

> Whatever the big picture – and this applies to both the learning and performing – there has to be a sense of 'now' about it. In learning, 'now' is more than concentration (which can even 'kill' the moment when it comes to the divergent thinking that characterises active learning); that place of being open to possibilities and progress. And, similarly, the 'now' of performing is about more than confirmation of those possibilities – for that's *far* too predictable a course to charter. It's the 'now' that needs to challenge the audience, and ultimately persuade it by means of convergent thinking. And all of this sets the scene for that magical moment when the combined 'now' of concentration and progression, confirmation and persuasion, blossom into communication: the ultimate musical 'now'. **Meurig Thomas**

Savouring the ambiguities

Pianists face a continual dilemma: we feel the urge to move away from the obvious in order to keep our playing vibrant and 'alive', and yet the further from the beaten track we stray, the more hazardous our playing could become. We hanker after innovation, but at the same time feel constrained by the *formalisation* seemingly evident from the score, by the conventions and complexities of historical performance practice, and ultimately by what critics, teachers or examiners may think about the choices we are making.

56 Peter Johnson argues that the score is at best a recipe of clues indicating what pianists *might* achieve, when it is surely more meaningful to examine what they *have* achieved. Johnson, P., 1997: 'Performance as Experience: The Problem of Assessment Criteria', in *British Journal of Music Education*, 14:3, p.276. Roy Howat (1995) also hints at the relationship between following a recipe and endeavouring to make sense of a musical score, here applied to the music of Chopin: 'Chopin's notation here reminds us that, like a cookbook, a musical score has two basic ways of indicating the recipe for a performance: either by the method "add fifty grams of flour" or by the method "add enough flour to achieve a smooth consistency"', p.7.
57 It goes without saying that we should take note of the composer's and editor's markings at every stage in our decision making – not as unthinking automatons, but as willing, mindful protagonists in the creation of a glorious musical moment.

Hence, we instinctively turn to those places in the music where we feel its open-endedness might permit a little freedom to creep in.

This brings us logically to a second, related perennial problem facing pianists as we attend to details: the issue of ambiguity. When is a *crescendo* not a *crescendo*? Answer: when it is an *allargando*. By this I simply mean that there may be instances in a score where a marking implies something rather different from its conventional meaning.[58] In this particular example a marked *crescendo* might be taken as a direction to ease back the pace of a climactic moment to heighten its splendour. Besides, composers rarely feel the need to mark in every detail, and thank goodness this is the case.[59] To varying degrees, it seems composers are prepared to confer trust in the pianist's capacity to read between the lines, and to piece together a workable strategy drawn from the signposts positioned around the page. Moreover, it seems a degree of ambiguity remains present in virtually all works of stature[60] – the presence of ambiguity permits multiple interpretations and leaves the door open to performers to stamp their mark.[61]

Having the courage of our convictions

Interpretation is really just a grand word for decision-making. Moreover, in piano music, subjectivity permeates the interpretive process at every conceivable stage. The mindful pianist's job is to mediate between whatever traces of the composer's thought processes remain evident and his/her own instincts. The loose ends of the pink ribbon then need tying up into a neat bow: the *performance*.

> A pianist's audience has to be convinced they are hearing sounds that are scientifically not possible, hence a pianist has also to be a magician! Other instrumentalists are able to change a note after it sounds, but unfortunately the pianist is denied this luxury. Nevertheless, somehow the pianist must persuade the audience that the large, unwieldy machine s/he is playing is capable of feeling and *breathing* with the music. To enable this to happen, the pianist needs to be creative with both horizontal and vertical voicing. Horizontal voicing is the relationship between a note and its next door neighbours on either side – we need to treat a melody as if it were a *vocalise* – and then there is vertical voicing, whereby the pianist must consider the importance of each note upwards within the chord. Finally, of course, there is the balance between these different elements. **Brian Ellsbury**

58 I once heard an eminent pianist state that ambiguous clues found in musical scores frequently amount to 'innuendos' – oblique markings which nevertheless require the pianist to connote clear meaning.

59 In contrast with this, take a glance at a piano score by Pierre Boulez (especially the Second and Third Sonatas) and you might wonder where on earth space permits the performer to exercise any decision-making at all.

60 Agawu, K., 1994: 'Ambiguity in tonal music: a preliminary study'. In A. Pople, ed., *Theory, Analysis and Meaning in Music* (Cambridge, Cambridge University Press), pp.86–107.

61 Janet Levy has argued that to deny the value of ambiguity in music is to reduce it to a clinical procedure devoid of imagination and significance: 'In general, much music theory and analysis has concerned itself with attempts to disambiguate ambiguous meanings of musical events or passages in which one or more interpretations appear possible. This is especially true in harmonic analysis, where the graphing and charting of harmonic progressions and voice leading are aided by arriving at a single unequivocal reading.' Levy, J., 'Beginning-Ending Ambiguity: Consequences of Performance Choices'. In Rink, J., *The Practice of Performance*, p.151.

The foolhardiest thing a performing pianist can do is to put off making decisions in a bid to minimise the risk of offending, or else in the misguided hope that the music will acquire meaning by osmosis. While we can never know what others hear in our interpretation, of one thing we can be certain – a chain of accurately played notes devoid of a sense of personal involvement will appear as cold as yesterday's sprouts. We need to be decisive and inventive with each and every key we depress, or the music is destined to remain as lifeless and undramatic as the page on which it was printed.

A *forte* marking at the start of a piece merely sets the environment in which the music might be encouraged to unfold – but it tells us little about which notes invite a subtle prising out within the melodic line, and less still about the chords enveloping it, how to balance dynamics effectively between the hands, or even how loud is 'loud'.[62] A humble *staccato* marking, of which there may be several hundred in a single movement of a sonata, will take on a different meaning according to the context in which it is found, just as a comma in a sentence may indicate a breath or pause to suggest the gravitas or intensity specific to the passage in question. As soon as it occurs to us to consider how fast, how loud or how smoothly we want a section to sound, we have embarked upon the rewarding but hugely challenging process of making decisions.

We may quickly realise that such decisions are contingent upon others we find ourselves making as we go along. For example, having chosen to play a phrase very loudly, we might discover that the tempo now needs to ease back a notch for entirely practical reasons of negotiating octaves or leaps. Or perhaps the *legato* line we have just spotted buried in the left hand notes of a piece by Schumann needs that extra bit of time to emerge persuasively, which implies a momentary relaxing of the pace. The score may, depending on whether it is by Scarlatti or Rachmaninov, appear more or less helpful in piecing together ideas of this sort; thankfully, it will never be the case that supreme diligence brings about attractive, impactful music.

Memorising

The older I become, the more I think that my memory has atrophied – that is certainly how I feel when trying to put anything new into the system! And yet, if asked to play something I haven't touched for more than 50 years, it generally reappears in full working order upon demand. As a child, I fully expected to be able to sight-read anything, and to play whatever it was from memory after a day or so – no *system*, just good fortune. Later, my analytical eye made larger pieces easier to memorise by having a minutely detailed understanding of a piece's construction, so anything from a Bach organ fugue to the Webern *Variations* was accommodated in the same way. Nowadays it's the same, just a bit harder! But I recommend a blend of the two methods: the more sight-

---

62 'Like many composers of the period, Mozart assumes that movements begin *forte* unless otherwise specified'. Levin, R.D., 2003: 'Performance practice in the music of Mozart', in *The Cambridge Companion to Mozart*, p.229 (Cambridge, Cambridge University Press).

reading you do, the better everything in your musical armoury becomes, and knowing precisely how the nuts and bolts are assembled in the act of composition helps wonderfully to order the brain. **Leslie Howard**

A 'head first' approach to the thorny business of memorising contrasts starkly with the tactic routinely taken by many pianists, perhaps especially younger ones, when first encountering a work, whereby the commitment to muscular memory becomes the all-important goal.[63] In some ways this resembles the piecing together of a dance routine in which successive repetitions lead to a second-nature grasp of what is needed.[64] It is as if by teaching the routine to the feet first, the dancer's conscious brain is given what it needs, too.[65]

At the heart of this (frequently perilous) finger-driven approach to memorising at the piano lies the entirely understandable desire to be free of the score at the earliest opportunity, so that fuller attention can be given to guiding the hands and fingers. It is often asserted that playing from memory super-stimulates the creative juices, though I remain circumspect on this matter.[66] Muscular memory is most certainly an indispensable component in fluid, convincing piano playing, but my contention is that unless used in conjunction with cerebral approaches, pianists walk a needlessly thin tightrope.[67]

One piece of practical advice concerning memorising is to learn, then memorise pieces in chunks from the back to the front, i.e. EDCBA, *not* ABCDE.[68] Memorising them in this way – and indeed practising skipping *forwards* to the part you just memorised when it comes to linking them up, means you save so much time when it comes to assembling the chunks together into twos, threes or fours. Many pianists memorise playing from A to B, then B to C etc., but when they get stuck they feel compelled to go back to A from B (or back to B from C, etc.). My method means you get into the habit of skipping forwards to the *next* section if you encounter a memory slip, always anticipating what is coming up next, not endlessly looping around the chunk that went astray. When you are able to restart a piece from anywhere, you really *know* it.

---

63 For a simply stunning display of human memory, we need look no further than Stephen Wiltshire, an autistic artist who managed to draw accurately the cityscapes of Tokyo (on a 52-foot canvas), Rome, Hong Kong, New York, Frankfurt, Madrid, Dubai, Jerusalem and London. He draws each city entirely from the memories stored away during brief helicopter rides. Interestingly, listening to music (pop and rock from the 70s–90s) always plays a significant part in the process; each of Wiltshire's sketches can take him up to a week to complete, and his work can be viewed at his permanent gallery in the Royal Opera Arcade, Pall Mall, London.

64 It seems the systematic cultivation of good habits averts the subconscious entrenchment of less good habits, hence some argue we ought not delay the process of memorising.

65 Interestingly, dancers do not seem to require their routines to be written down – i.e. the equivalent of a musical score.

66 In his later years on stage, Sviatoslav Richter (1915–1997) wisely chose to play increasingly with the score; this does not appear to have impacted negatively on his playing. One of the most moving Mozart concerto performances I have ever heard was given by the recently deceased Bernard Roberts (1933–2013), who despite having performed the work many times, elected to read from a score. Clifford Curzon (1907–82) and Dame Myra Hess (1890–1965) also frequently preferred to play from scores.

67 If only pianists could feel a little happier about distancing themselves from the compulsion to memorise – just think of the amount of extra repertoire we would feel happy to perform in public.

68 As Paul Comeau recommends, we should learn more extended pieces back to front (even if we have no intention of 'formally' memorising it), if only to head off the risk of 'performance crumble' syndrome.

7 Useful tips for mindful practising

Oiling the wheels of progress

> Rehearse every hand movement precisely, like a ballet dancer. Spot the most challenging passages and work at these first. Don't overdo separate hands practice (although LH, RH, LH can be useful: almost always work from the bass upwards). If the whole piece is challenging, start in different places, but particularly work from the end backwards; always lead from the *less*-known to the known. In leaps, don't attempt to play the note you are leaping to before you have perfected the hand/arm preparatory movement. Give 90 percent of attention to preparatory and follow-through movements and the notes will largely look after themselves. You might try leaving out certain notes on purpose, or even adding extra ones in. Avoid mechanically going around the same passage too many times – on the other hand, it can be invaluable to play something very short perfectly 20 times in a row; doing this can save a lot of time in the long term. **Paul Comeau**

Here are some tips, in no particular order, for mindful practice:

- You wouldn't choose a day when you've got backache to dig out your potato patch, so why would you put yourself through tortuous activities in the practice room when you are not feeling up to it? Being kind to yourself is not being 'slack', it is being mindful of how you are feeling and responding sensibly. There are days when you feel your playing is invincible; there will also be days when you simply need to reaffirm your connection to the instrument.

- Move fluidly from one 'event' to the next in your practice session without excessive recourse to the clock or some unrealistic timeframe.[69] Keep your mind alive and in a state of vivid expectation.

- Enjoy the freedom to be random from time to time. There is an important distinction to be made between randomness and aimlessness.

- Listen to your inner voice, but don't always feel compelled to obey it. There is a middle line to be drawn between having an agenda you broadly intend to follow and feeling free to respond to the whim of the moment.

- Leave the book open to your favourite page of a piece you are currently working on, so that each time you walk past the piano you reinforce your positive feeling for it.

- Be creative with every minute of your practising. Try not to lapse into mindless regurgitation by continually feeding yourself ways of keeping

---

69 It is important to resist the urge to micro-manage your time; broad, sensible objectives are good to have in mind, but flexibility is a key attribute of efficient practising.

stimulated. Putting a cat among the pigeons occasionally does not have to result in a cloud of feathers – if something bizarrely illuminating occurs to you while practising, run with it. The key is to be alive to all possibilities.

- Practise taking risks – the floor won't swallow you up. Daring to step outside of your normal approach is your only hope of stumbling across something new and inspirational in your playing.

- If you feel yourself starting to get bored, you may actually be running low on energy. Either way, distract yourself by channelling your attention into some new activity in order to regain interest and focus.

- Try not to beat yourself up if your playing appears not to be progressing as you had hoped it might. Besides, you may not be objective in maligning your efforts – put your assessment on hold and see how you feel about it tomorrow.

- Practising slowly, *forte*, and with very decisive finger action (crucially, with relaxed wrists), is an excellent method of 'reconnecting' with your technique if you start to feel that your playing is becoming superficial.

- Refrain from continually rewinding to the beginning of a piece when practising – target specific places which demand attention and approach these with as many different methods as you dare.

- In yoga, bending motions are often followed by opposing movements to ensure freedom and flexibility are maintained, as well as necessary relaxation of the muscle groups. In piano playing, something similar is to be highly recommended – ten minutes of practising music that requires a lot of stretching calls for intermittent gentle clenching of the fist to counteract it, and shaking of the wrist with the arm hanging down by your side.

- Keep things fresh. Practise *legato* passages *staccato*, slow-moving music quickly, quiet music loudly, and so on. These sorts of activities instantly rejuvenate the brain and may even add a new twist to your technical resources.

- Challenge yourself to do something, then set about doing it, but be prepared to adapt as you go along; pause frequently to take stock of what is actually happening.

- When practising lyrical passages, try breathing as you would if you were singing them – literally in the same places – this promotes a sense of musical progression and can at the same time cause you to reconsider the *speed* at which you have been taking the music.

- In passages which cause the hand to adopt unusual or distorted shapes, especially in highly chromatic music, take a moment to inspect your wrist and fingers to ensure you are not placing unrealistic demands on yourself. If necessary, rethink the hand shape and get into the habit of self-policing what you are doing. You might even practise the trickier hand shapes away from the piano – often of course, it is not the trickiness of a particular hand shape that is the chief concern, it is getting to it or from it.

- Experiment with playing left hand music in the right, and vice versa. This adds a frisson of daringness to the practising, but more importantly it can alleviate issues of insecure coordination or asynchrony between the hands. This activity will also immediately flag up any notes that have not been reliably learned. Something similar can be achieved by transposing the entire passage into distant keys – a skill organists learn from quite early on.

- Many teachers advocate the singing of one part while playing the other. Clearly the context will determine the relevance of such an approach (there is perhaps little to be gained from singing an Alberti bass, for example).

- When considering the precise function of the pedal, it pays to think of what singers and other instrumentalists are routinely called upon to do: string players lift the bow when creating musically defined gestures, just as 'breathing' musicians must intelligently position their choice of breathing places so as not to undermine the integrity of the musical line. Thought of in this way, lifting the pedal (and even the hands a fraction) achieves something remarkably similar.[70]

- Keep enjoyment of what you are doing foremost in your mind. This need not be in conflict with fulfilling your longer-term objectives, as long as these are both realistic and flexible enough to accommodate subtle changes of direction.

- Your emotional intelligence counts for more than playing devil's advocate to your intellect. Listen to it, trust it and be prepared to shift course if you really feel strongly that something is not working for you.

- Your playing is only your *playing* – it does not 'define' you. If you have found it hard to rise above a particularly challenging objective, resist the notion that you are a failure.

- Do not let your chief attributes become your biggest stumbling blocks. For example, although it is undoubtedly good to be able to anchor your pulse in much piano music, being too fixed or 'metronomic' about it will render your playing predictable, shapeless and unexciting. The reason we want to fix a solid pulse is to earn the right elsewhere to do as we see fit.[71]

- Beware of 'small room' syndrome. Playing for extended periods in a small practice room can hem you into an overly precious dynamic palette. We need to project, even when playing *pianissimo*.[72] Imagine yourself playing in a larger space and expect to hear a big, assertive sound; this invariably means ratcheting up your *overall* dynamic range by a couple of notches.

---

70 Remembering to breathe while playing can feel almost as rejuvenating as taking a power-nap! Steady breathing (pianists often hold their breath) keeps the brain refuelled and regulates the heart rate; it also helps to prevent hurrying when performing and permits the music itself to 'breathe'.

71 Beate Popperwell, Professor at the RWCMD in the 1980s, reportedly said of Brahms's piano music: 'most Brahms is in $\frac{3}{4}$ time; if not, it may as well be' (my thanks to Brian Ellsbury for passing on that little gem).

72 Even though one of the first things we learn as pianists is that the piano is a percussion instrument, most of us seem to have forgotten this within a day. Any percussion instrument needs a decisive strike to make it work properly; the piano will never respond positively to a prod, tickle or jab.

This is especially true when practising pieces which are quiet virtually all of the way through, for example, Debussy's *Canope*.[73]

- In my experience, people settle on a tempo far too quickly when learning a new piece. Though we can all feel more at ease with our facility when playing at a particular speed, unless we remain alive to the possibility of something different we can never know if we have made the best decision.

- Put yourself in harm's way from time to time. Say yes to accompanying someone at short notice, even without knowing what the commitment entails. Agree to perform at your local piano club, or at a summer school, and celebrate the courage you showed in doing so. Little steps such as these can have an immeasurable impact on your level of confidence and sense of accomplishment, all of which will trickle into your playing in positive ways.

- Warm up your mind, body and fingers before you settle down to periods of intense practice. Then decide for yourself roughly how long each session should be and don't overrun by too much. Whereas children often benefit from a set time of day, and a fairly regimented amount of time, to keep them on the straight and narrow, adults usually need to be more flexible. Don't be beguiled into counting up the hours like rings on a tree – think also about the optimal gap between your sessions. Many people respond more positively to several brief encounters than one gargantuan effort – there needs to be time to digest. There seems little point in flogging on with a practice session if your fingers are hurting or if your brain has started to turn into fried Camembert.

- Aim not to become too much of a slave to habit. Shake things up by changing the way you approach your daily practising – try different times of the day, before or after food or sleep, in the dark, by candlelight, in an empty house, a full house, with joss-sticks or with the window open. Getting the lighting right, and paying attention to the *feng shui* of your room, might just tip the balance in favour of more productive practice sessions.

- Experiment regularly with the things you might otherwise take for granted in your playing. This could include reconsidering fingering choices if certain complicated patterns haven't quite jelled as you had hoped, or practising fast right-hand passages down in the bass register.

- Fixing too rigidly on aspects of dynamics, articulation and pedalling mitigates the possibility for changes of overall strategy, so revisit these regularly – use a pencil, not a pen, if you want to keep your options open. Question why you are doing something – is it actually working?

- Running is not fast walking. Just as the muscles we use to walk are quite different from those we use to run, playing the piano quickly is wholly different from playing slowly. For this reason, fingering choices sometimes need a complete rethink when envisaged for the plodding pace at which they were more than likely conceived.

73 The dynamics in Debussy's *Canope*, from Preludes Book 2, rarely rise above *piano*. Indeed, in the Durand 1913 edition of this 33-bar piece there are no fewer than 32 instances of *piano* or *pianissimo*.

- Don't practise out of a sense of duty to yourself. Notwithstanding those occasions where you need to knuckle down prior to an exam or other event, it is better to miss a practice session than emerge from one in a catatonic rage.

- Expect your playing to improve and there is a strong chance that it will. A positive attitude can carry you through temporary blips in productivity (and even inactivity).

- Confidence in what you're doing is a vital component in your motivation as a pianist. Confidence only turns the corner into arrogance when it is misplaced; bear in mind that practising is as much about building trust in your own capabilities as it is about sorting out pesky problems with double-sharps or cross-rhythms.

- Vary the pace at which you allow yourself to absorb the surface details in a score. Not unlike speed-reading a book, it is possible to scan the pages swiftly to get an overall feel for what is coming your way; then ease the pace to achieve a more considered survey.

- Break the habits which might lead to negative energy in the practice room. A cocktail of unhealthy thoughts – *'I'll never manage this, it's far too difficult…why can't I play this up to speed?'* – may well lead to an adverse emotional reaction and uproot the very thing we are endeavouring to achieve.

- In one of his excellent online videos, Josh Wright (an American pianist who has his own YouTube Channel) demonstrates what he calls the '4321' method of practising. In brief, you play a tricky fast passage but repeat each note within it (in both hands) four times, then three, and so on, in a kind of ever-shortening stutter, to really reinforce the relative placing of notes in the mind and fingers. A good workout for the wrists, too.

- Before you can hope to achieve a rapport with an audience, it is necessary to establish a rapport with yourself. In practical terms, this amounts to being enchanted by the music you are producing, but not becoming overwhelmed. Like all aspects of piano playing, this needs thoughtful practice and, importantly, an ability to hear yourself as others do.

- From time to time, unbottle your creative juices: 'If you run fast enough, you effectively run out of your body into a space that only belongs to you…you are unassailable.'[74]

- It is natural when practising (and even performing, under certain circumstances) to vacillate between feeling like a small child and a superhero. Attuning to these potentially derailing pendulum-swings is all part of coming to terms with yourself, first as a human being and then as a pianist.

- When practising just prior to an event of some kind, keep in mind that you will be attempting to create something that is greater and more enduring than yourself. A good performance is like a puff of expensive perfume – it can linger in the listener's memory long after the event itself has passed.

---

74 Ines Geipel, Sociologist and former world-class runner, in 'Attention: A life in Extremes', Netflix, 2016.

- In one sense, practising comes down to an ongoing exercise in risk-containment. We weigh up what seems possible or desirable, balance this with what feels practicable, then commit to the music with all the enthusiasm and vitality we can muster.

- Get into the right mood before practising a tempestuous piece: go for a jog in the rain, or perhaps have a swim before practising some Debussy…

One of the most difficult aspects of playing the piano for many people is achieving independence when coordinating the hands in complex passagework. Even if you can play each hand separately with perfect ease and control, trouble can then arise assembling them if you cannot hear how one hand may be inadvertently compromising the other. A great practice tip Cyril Smith gave me serves as a sort of 'halfway house', whereby you can be physically playing hands-together while only *hearing* one hand. To do this, simply play one hand on the keyboard as normal, while the other one plays on the frame or music desk above the keyboard. This can be particularly helpful when practising polyrhythms or when you want to hear exactly what one hand is doing while accompanying a melody in the other.

Another useful practice tip for polyrhythms is occasionally to adopt a 'reverse' thought-process. Instead of trying to fit the notes precisely between your hands, imagine that you are in fact trying to play them together but just slightly 'failing'. I find that this approach can be especially helpful in Chopin when I want to make complex polyrhythms sound more natural and flowing, and less contrivedly 'fitted'.

When a student's fingerwork sounds overly heavy, and they are struggling to achieve clarity in certain passages, I sometimes suggest they pretend they are playing *staccato*, but without their fingers actually leaving the keys. This 'imagined' *staccato* can help give fingerwork an irresistible clarity of articulation, or *jeu perlé* touch, and can sometimes even help to unstick trills. **Margaret Fingerhut**

Part 3

Performing

8 Achieving intensity

Intensity: The engine of music

The sum of all the structural, stylistic and characterful clues we are able to glean from a score, coupled with our poetic insights and vision for the shape and trajectory the music presents to us, can be thought of as its intensity, its engine or lifeblood. As a pianist, the very word 'intensity'[75] has always implied to me an emotional force or propulsion forwards.[76] One might prefer to think of intensity as a clumping together of discrete elements, a snowball of musical energy tumbling downhill, gathering up further elements, qualities and momentum all the while. Think how Chopin's Nocturnes typically develop – serene music triggers a prolonged *agitato* (quasi-development) section, before finally returning us to a state of sublime tranquillity. Intensity is often traceable from the score alone and will most definitely be audible in a good performance, be it live or recorded. In 19th century repertoire in particular the ebb and flow of intensity might readily be seen to function at a structural level, even one as unsurprising as ternary form.[77] In pieces which appear structurally ambiguous there may still be a palpable intensity which morphs, absorbs and reflects the uneven terrain it moves over.

Intensity is not just what transports the music though, it is what subsequently impels – and *compels* – the pianist and the listener in equal measure. Actually, I believe intensity is what powers a composition from the moment of its inception; it is already 'there', just as the pianist is, ready and waiting to go. We are instinctively aware of this energy as it twists, turns, eddies and swells, journeying the music in a direction particular to itself. But it falls upon the mindful pianist to galvanise this pent up tension and then effect a controlled release in the moment of performance.

If the music needs to pack a punch, then its intensity may take the form of sustained power and a declamatory impact, whereas if we decide the music

---

75 Intensity in music can be understood to mean many different things. In the simplest terms, it could reflect certain structural properties discernible from a score, those performance elements brought to bear by the performer (the 'playing' itself, but also body movement, expressions etc.), the context in which these things are unfolding (concert hall or recorded performance) and of course what the listener perceives it all to mean. John Rink's use of intensity curves are of immense value in this regard, and indeed have certainly influenced my approach in the coming 'potted' analyses. 'John Rink's 'intensity curves'…provide a summary representation of multiple musical parameters and so facilitate the real-time pacing of performance.' Cook, N., 2013: *Beyond the Score: Music as Performance* (Oxford, Oxford University Press), p.78. 'Much of his [Rink's] work has focused on the notion of 'intensity' and upon how the performer might seek it.' King, E., Gritten, A., Ed., 2006: *Music and Gesture* (Oxford, Routledge), p.215.

76 Familiar musical structures can show up as a series of conspicuous 'peaks and troughs' from which moments of significance appear illuminated – enabling us to see the wood for the trees. Expressed in this way, a composer's employment of register, dynamics, tempo variation and intensity may be seen to embody some underlying directional function. In connecting with the composer's motives one takes a step closer to acquiring a meaningful global conception, which might even ease the process of memorisation. This seems especially pertinent in piano music, where notational minutiae can so easily distract the pianist from what is important.

77 Ternary form is ubiquitous in music throughout the past two hundred years. Ternary form can be seen as underpinning the arch shape in a work such as a sonata or concerto; even the faintest whiff of ternary form can be enough to give a welcome sense of closure to a musical work.

leans towards a more intimate sentiment, or one of quiet contemplation, then its intensity may be found languishing elsewhere in its serenest corners.[78] There is a kind of alchemy at work when the pianist is able to harness all these fragments of musical energy. If a performance stands out by virtue of its daringly reimagined tempo, for example, we may immediately sense a shift in the music's intensity – perhaps to its perceived advantage, perhaps not.[79] From the pianist's perspective, our pursuit of intensity may cause us to focus on dynamics in a particular piece, its ever-changing temporal dimensions, or of course both simultaneously – these are, after all, the two foremost 'pillars' of piano playing which come under our direct influence.[80]

Alternatively, we might choose to allow the piano, the hall or even the audience to influence our decisions in ways we could not have predicted when practising alone at home. In other words, we can bring intensity to our playing, consciously and emphatically, or feel it being drawn out of us by 'mysterious' forces beyond our cognitive control. In some instances, we are not entirely sure how we managed to convey the mood or atmosphere of a piece as successfully as we did, and indeed there are many who would assert that it does not actually matter: just let the music release itself and be done with it.[81]

Plan, then play

The problem with sidestepping inquiry into how or why pianists do what we do is that this renders our playing – and our hit-rate when on stage or in an exam room – more random and mutable than it needs to be. Besides, one does not have to be an 'analytically-minded' pianist to be a mindful pianist. We practise in order to increase the chance of homing in on what we have decided the music amounts to, and then resolve to tease it out when we find ourselves in a variety of environments. Replication might not be a component of piano

78 Intensity might take the form of spine-tinglingly hushed, seemingly inert piano music, for example *Le Gibet*, from Ravel's *Gaspard de la nuit*. Or it can seem terrifyingly lugubrious and ominous, like the opening moments in Scriabin's Second Sonata – in both cases it is especially important to keep the music trickling forward purposefully in order to preserve its intensity.
79 Some pianists of the modern age, notably Ivo Pogorelich and Lang Lang, seem to delight in extremes of tempo. The habits of the so-called *enfant terrible* will inevitably divide the crowd, but that is arguably better than boring them.
80 Tobias Matthay's earnest and sincere desire to incorporate tonal variety within the scope of artistic pianism appears questionable in the light of evidence provided by many empirical studies from as early as the 1930s. 'It makes no difference whether the key is struck by an accelerating, retarding, even, or any form of irregular movement; the only significant thing the player controls in the stroke is the velocity of the key at the exact moment that it throws off the hammer...The elaborate care taken in the development of form, weight, pressure, and rate of arm, wrist, and finger movements is fully justified insofar as it results in a refined control of the intensity of the tone, but not for any independent change in tone *quality*...It reduces touch to the fundamental factor of intensity' (Seashore, *Psychology of Music*, 1936, p.227).
    There is, however, much of value still to be gained from reading Matthay's theories on piano technique; many pianists from the early part of the 20th century owe their solid technical foundation to Matthay's dedicated pedagogy (Myra Hess in particular), but presumably there are as many for whom the old chestnut of *tonal* variety remains as pertinent as ever. Louis Kentner (1905–1987), for example, stated: 'It is indeed possible to make an ugly, harsh noise – no one will deny that. That it is also possible to create a beautiful sound (within the limitation of each instrument), and that there are differences of touch – not merely those of loud and soft – is a matter of practical experience which everyone who has ears to hear will be aware of, no matter how difficult or impossible it might be to prove it scientifically'. Kentner, L., 1984: *Piano*, (Kahn & Averill), p.80.
81 The term 'flow state' has become ubiquitous in mindfulness circles to coin something not wholly dissimilar to what I am describing in more specifically musical terms: 'intensity'.

playing we care to think about as we perform for ourselves or others, yet I would argue we are to an appreciable extent reliving our pre-dreamed dream, not drifting into some torpid hallucination while sat at the piano. Implicit in this is that we apply our conscious minds as well as our innate instincts to the music as we caress it into life through the medium of our fingers. We need to be in control, not just of our movements, but the destiny of the music itself.[82]

If we become beguiled into thinking spontaneity is all that matters in our performances, we might be too easily swayed from pursuing clear objectives when practising.[83] Practising is about working through the possibilities the music presents to us and melding these with what we feel we are able to bring to it in physical and emotional ways. We need to grasp what it is we wish to achieve with a piece of music in order to play with consistency and confidence. It is of course true that our ideas should respond and adapt over time, but they cannot be permitted to bend with every variant in wind direction. Music, however brief and unprepossessing it may be, is never one 'thing', so we must feel its undulations with every passing phrase and be willing to resonate with it in the ways we feel convinced will be most helpful. We of course need to be spontaneous, but only insofar as the music itself is able to tolerate it.

We must seek out intensity in every musical gesture if the work as a whole is to acquire meaning and momentum. But how will we know it when we see it, or indeed hear it? Here are one or two alternative ways of searching out intensity in a new piece.

Rachmaninov, Prelude in D Op.23 No.4

Can there really be a better example of unbridled intensity in piano music than this Rachmaninov Prelude? For a small-scale work lasting around four minutes, its overall trajectory is utterly compelling; indeed the music's sense of arrival, or its 'emotional climax',[84] gathers up into epic proportions.

This rather special climactic moment is positioned exactly two-thirds of the way into the piece, at bar 51. We can gain an insight into how Rachmaninov achieves this so satisfyingly by spotlighting three separate aspects of the Prelude readily observable in the score.[85] I invite you to don your analytical hat for just a moment, to see how captivatingly the composer knits together these score elements.

---

82 A performance represents the pianist's 'reward' for all that practising: a chance to turn multiple possibilities into a one-off, memorable reality.
83 Interestingly, Arthur Rubinstein's natural flair as a young man caused him to skim over learning the repertoire. This was to his later regret; in his late forties Rubinstein had a change of heart and courageously decided to put in up to nine hours' practice a day, thereby effectively relearning his entire repertoire from scratch.
84 In contemporary music analysis this is sometimes referred to as the 'expressive high-point' or 'goal' in Romantic pieces. Incidentally, in performances, the climax also appears almost exactly two-thirds in; for example, Richter places his climax sixty-three percent of the way through a performance lasting 4:14. Other examples of high-points are numerous in Rachmaninov's oeuvre, but notably the middle movements of the Concerto No.2 and No.3; it also functions palpably in a number of works by Liszt, for example *Liebestod* (Transcription on 'Tristan und Isolde') and the Sonata in B minor. Tanner, M., Autumn 2000: 'The Power of Performance as an Alternative Analytical Discourse: The Liszt Sonata in B Minor', *19th Century Music*, Vol. 24 No.2, 173–192.
85 As well as dynamics, register and density, it is conceivable in some instances to quantify other surface details found in a score, such as tempo markings, phrasing and even articulation.

Rachmaninov, Prelude in D Op.23 No.4, bb.50–52

Allow me first to walk you through Rachmaninov's use of **dynamics** in the Prelude. The composer unfolds his overall scheme with patience and farsightedness (the piece ends wrapped up in the sublime comfort blanket of D major, just as it began, marked *pianissimo*); indeed, from the dynamics alone there cannot be the slightest doubt where the music is headed during the course of its 77 bars. A graphic representation of dynamics is shown below;[86] essentially, this graph reveals several distinctive peaks, which build like stepping-stones towards and away from the conspicuous climax, marked *fortissimo*.[87] Note how, at bar 47, Rachmaninov marks an abrupt *drop* in dynamic to *piano*, which serves to accentuate the 'big moment' arriving four bars later; secondly, the composer builds in what could be described as a dynamic 'aftershock', marked *forte*, positioned ten bars after the climax at bar 61. The function of this, I suggest, is to preserve the music's last vestiges of white-hot intensity, rather than simply allow it to fizzle out like a spent firework.

Rachmaninov, Prelude in D Op. 23 No. 4: dynamics

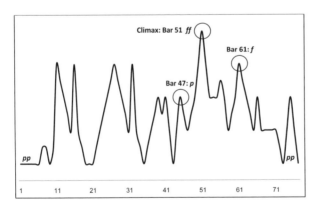

Next, let us consider the '**density**' of the Prelude, by which I am referring to the aggregated number of notes occurring in each bar – the 'note traffic' in the piece, if you like. From the graph below, a pronounced peak can be seen to coincide precisely with the dynamic peak.

---

86   The graph quantifies dynamics on a bar-by-bar basis, taking values from *pianissimo* to *fortissimo* and all the conventional shades therein.

87   In simplified terms, this doubly-suspended E minor chord fits into an overall scheme: II V I.

Rachmaninov, Prelude in D Op. 23 No. 4: density

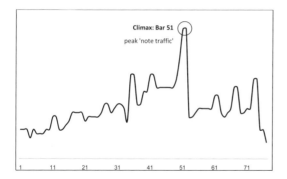

Finally, there is the '**registral**' behaviour of the music. This is a representation of the intervallic gap existing between the highest and lowest notes in each bar of the piece.[88] Once again, the graph reveals a compelling peak at bar 51, where the hands find themselves spaced apart by five and a half octaves.

Rachmaninov, Prelude in D Op. 23 No. 4: register

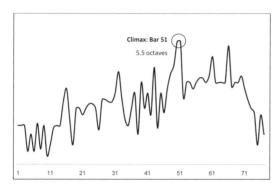

Importantly, the precise intersection of these three score aspects – dynamics, density and register – also frequently coincides with what expert pianists *actually* seem driven to achieve in their performances. Indeed, from a purely acoustic evaluation, the emotional swell readily detectable often increases considerably in this region of the music, and then drops off conspicuously thereafter. Moreover, for many pianists, the music's grander gestures seem to rely upon a somewhat elastic view of tempo.[89]

It is perhaps even easier to understand how all this comes together meaningfully if we amalgamate all three aspects into a single graph, below; this, in spirit, is not dissimilar to what John Rink has called 'the piece in a nutshell'.[90] I am not suggesting that the structural functions deducible

88 It seems clear that as piano music intensifies, composers like to expand the texture by employing the extremes of the keyboard 'orchestrally' and hence widen the registral space that exists between the hands. The sustain pedal commonly heightens the effect further.
89 'While playing, the performer engages in a continual dialogue between the comprehensive architecture and the 'here-and-now', between some sort of goal-directed impulse at the uppermost level (the piece 'in a nutshell') and subsidiary motions extending down to the beat or sub-beat level, with different parts of the hierarchy activated at different points within the performance'. Rink J., 1999: *Translating Musical Meaning: The Nineteenth Century Performer as Narrator.* In N. Cook & M. Everist (eds.), 'Rethinking Music' (Oxford, Oxford University Press), pp.217–38.

from Rachmaninov's Prelude amount to unassailable evidence of how we must go about *playing* the piece, yet empirical approaches of this kind are potentially of great value to pianists, especially perhaps those coming to the music afresh.[91]

Rachmaninov, Prelude in D Op. 23 No. 4: overview

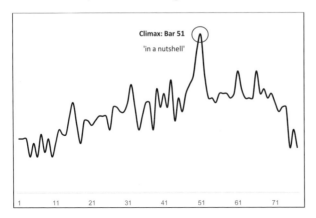

Re-composing a piece

If it is reasonable to suggest that the composer should be mindful of the performer's perspective, surely the opposite point is open for discussion? The more willing the pianist is to enter into the spirit of the compositional process, the easier and more natural it will be to turn all those dots into pleasurable music. Giving a performance its 'legs' unquestionably involves a degree of compositional instinct. With this in mind, I thought I would share with you an approach I have been using in my teaching for a number of years: I call it (provocatively) 're-composing a piece'. The motivation, I hasten to add, is not to make the piece 'better', or 'fix' perceived shortcomings, nor is it to declare open season on a piece which works magnificently well exactly as it is, for that would be farcical. Rather, the point is to engage more naturally with the music's fundamental intensity and thereby gain an interesting vantage point. This is perhaps akin to viewing a painting from several different angles in the hope of glimpsing an aspect we had not considered before. I will give you one brief practical example, though you will doubtless see how the approach could work equally well in a variety of pieces from different idioms.

Bach, Prelude in C Minor, BWV 847 Bk.1

Bach's Prelude from his Prelude and Fugue in C Minor, when played imaginatively with fingers of steel and wrists of rubber, dances athletically through a variety of complex harmonic patterns and sequences in pursuit of

90 This graph constitutes an 'averaging' of the first three as described, i.e. an 'idealisation' to show the music's core intensity, based on Rachmaninov's use of dynamics, register and density.

91 Nor, incidentally, am I suggesting that Rachmaninov started out with such a scheme 'formally' in mind, merely that his instinctive processes (which will doubtless have tapped into his intuitions as a virtuoso performer) led him to compose in this way.

its even racier *Presto* section near the end. In fact, what makes the piece so remarkable – and, in the right hands, truly electric – is its sense of journey to the unknown.[92]

Bach, Prelude from Prelude and Fugue in C Minor, BWV 847, Bk. 1, bb. 1–2

Unfortunately, some pianists appear inclined to rattle through the semiquavers with a cavalier disinterest in the music's intriguing undulations and modulations, so that the only thing left to admire (possibly) is evenness of fingerwork.[93] For a performance to impact more tellingly, it needs the kind of care we would give it had we composed the piece ourselves. So that is precisely what I am suggesting we attempt to do.

When we think how effective Gounod's *Ave Maria* sounds when glued onto Bach's Prelude in C Major, from Book 1 of the '48', we glimpse at what might be achievable with its minor key distant nephew. My feeling is that we learn a great deal about the potency of Bach's creation by being daringly creative ourselves. This is a somewhat lateral approach, but certainly one which is likely to be more lucrative than churning through it endlessly in the hope of divine inspiration. From it, we may gain a clearer insight into Bach's harmonic scheme as well as, perhaps, an inkling of its intensity. The result, given below, is simply an impression of the music's potential to become something more personal to me, dreamed up in a matter of minutes – it is by no means the final word on embellishment, more a discussion point.

In my re-composed version below, the left hand's notes are exactly as provided by the composer. However, instead of meshing in yet more semiquavers for the right hand to play throughout, as Bach did to tremendous effect, I have dared to trade the harpsichord-type texture for a melody, quasi Gounod.[94] Why not play it through and see what you might have done with it? I found myself taking liberties with dynamics and even a little articulation, purely in response to the 'new' music I was adding.

92 In music which 'journeys' so daringly, we seem able to put to one side what we already know will happen, a little like watching a re-run of a favourite TV comedy show and still finding ourselves laughing at the punchlines.

93 There is so much more lying in wait for us when interpreting Baroque keyboard music than simply following the more obvious possibilities for terraced dynamics or pulling off a predictable *rallentando* at a *tierce de Picardie*. The 'typewriter' approach evident in some amateur performances is perhaps a symptom of a hypnotic effect induced by long chains of semiquavers.

94 For a fully worked-out piano transcription of Bach's Cello Suite No.1 in G major BWV 1007, see my Praeludium in 'Listen to the World' Book 5, Spartan Press SP1225.

Bach, Prelude from Prelude and Fugue in C Minor, BWV 847, 'recomposed'

If nothing else, one certainly gains a more robust grasp of Bach's harmonic impetus. I feel this approach to be particularly helpful in 'busy' or *toccata*-type keyboard music where there is no pre-existing melody as such to cling onto, as is the case here. Ultimately of course, we must accede to Bach's writing, though as a composer-pianist I might hazard a guess that Bach would have been more than willing to entertain brief detours of this kind. Moreover, were Bach to have been more melodically motivated when composing this prelude, and not inclined to arouse us with a million notes, I have little doubt the result would have been more striking than my own. But this is hardly the point: my reinvention brought me that little step closer to Bach's invention.

The organic score: Music in a nutshell

Here is another tactic you might wish to consider if you are keen to gain a clearer understanding of how a piece 'works' at its core level. Not unlike the previous activity – 're-composing a piece' – you are being invited to take a tangential approach. It is theoretical only insofar as it will require you to be methodical, however the process itself is heavily instinctive. In essence, you will be taking a pre-existing score, whittling it down to its skeleton state and considering afresh the information you are left with.

I have used this approach extensively, both in groups and with players of different ages and levels during the past twenty years or more. Many pianists have found it to be an eye-opening experience, even those whose playing is at a comparatively rudimentary stage. Indeed, you will quickly see how creating and working with your own 'organic score' can be equally enlightening, whether applied to a grade 1 piece or a lengthy concert item spilling over with complexities. Importantly, you will learn something about yourself as you gain confidence in freeing up your more creative side. The whole process will certainly awaken the detective in you, but in a more practical way it can bring you a step or two closer to the composer, who of course may once have done something similar with the original manuscript.[95] You will be hunting for patterns and inconsistencies dotted about the page, spotting high-points and noticing places where there appears to be a gathering together of potentially interesting surface details.

How, might you ask, can this approach help me to play a Chopin prelude or a Scarlatti sonata? Organic scores force us to become more cognisant of what we

---

95 Admittedly, composers may well introduce 'expressive' markings at the same time as constructing the score itself (adding weight to the view that expressive markings can function structurally), rather than after the event. Either way, there is surely something organic about the creation of virtually any musical score.

are doing.[96] I suggested earlier that the first step towards making sense of any score is to invest something of ourselves into it. But this can seem strangely counterintuitive when we are faced with a plethora of composer's markings or an ominous weight of authoritative editorial commentary. In reality of course, even the most elaborate looking score is nothing but ink and paper until it is nudged into life by a living, breathing musician, and this is where the mindful pianist's input becomes indispensable.

Creating an organic score

1 Using a copyright-free online resource, such as IMSLP, print off the score and paint out every 'expressive' marking present – articulation, dynamics, changes in tempo, phrase marks and indeed anything else you would normally latch onto for help with building an interpretation, so only notes and rhythms remain – then make a copy.[97]

2 Now scan and print out your 'skeleton' version and file it away for a week or two; try to resist taking a peek.[98]

3 Make your first pass of the music sat at the kitchen table – preferably not anywhere near the piano. Pencil in some provisional thoughts about phrasing, dynamics and so on, pausing regularly to replay the music in your head if you can.[99]

4 Next, perched at the piano, your homemade score will appear oddly bereft of 'musical' information – even a piece by Brahms might at first glance resemble the slow movement of a Haydn sonata. With a coloured pen, make sure you mark in your ideal metronome marking, for none of the decisions you make will be more indicative of musical character than the tempo.[100] As we mull over the prospects for adding phrasing and articulation, the *dynamics* of dynamics takes on a new and powerful meaning, too.[101] We may feel inclined to scribble in a *rallentando* here and an *a tempo* there, or perhaps to draw in arrows back and forth as I have done in the two examples below to illustrate the motion and recession of intensity.

Not all of your initial pencilled-in ideas will make sense, now that you are able to try them out at the instrument, though this is of course in the very nature of any organic process; it adapts. You can feel free to make any changes you see fit in light of the practicalities of having to place fingers on keys, for it has now

---

96 They are also an excellent way of reigniting a spark of interest in a piece you played years ago and with which you wish to reacquaint yourself.

97 If you are able to use a digital pen (Surface Pro or iPad Pro), this process is surprisingly expeditious when working with a scanned PDF version of the score.

98 Ideally, you would be working with scores someone else created for you (why not create some for a friend or colleague to use, and effect a swap, taking due account of each other's playing level). Doing this would mean that the style and character of the piece is also off limits, since you would not necessarily know who the composer is or the work's title when encountering a skeleton score.

99 The process itself can help to bridge the gap between the visual presence of the score and one's aural grasp of the music.

100 In my experience, pianists tend to attach themselves like glue to their initial choice of tempo, which effectively precludes interpretive growth further down the line. What is comfortable for the pianist is not necessarily comfortable for the music.

101 I recommend you read Neil Todd's enlightening paper. Todd, N., 1992: 'The dynamics of dynamics: a model of musical expression', in *Journal of the Acoustical Society of America*, 91, 3540–3550.

effectively become *your* piece. You are permitting yourself a certain largesse in order to learn something about what makes *you* tick, not just the music.

After just a few minutes of thoughtful study and a few daring strokes of the pen, the music in front of you bristles with possibilities. In its present state, dare to live with your version of the piece for a little while longer. Play it through a number of times more and perhaps present it to a few friends. Finesse your newly marked-up organic score as much as you like, then return to it a few days' later, once your mind has settled; it is important to create a little distance between yourself and the process you have just been through. Record yourself playing the piece, keeping as close as possible to what you have annotated.

A number of students with whom I have shared this approach seem never to have felt the burden of interpretation so acutely before. A few even feel a certain queasiness at having dared to meddle with the music of an esteemed composer. And yet, when we stop to think of it, this is precisely what we do every time we sit down to *play* music composed by someone else. However hard we may endeavour to honour the surface details in a revered work, it seems we are compelled to decipher, ameliorate and illuminate the score in every bar. Active interpretation is not just a vague possibility for pianists to ponder on, it is fundamental to the craft of performing.

This should give us pause for thought as we finally get around to comparing the printed score alongside our own 'idealised' version.[102] Aim to make this more than merely a game of spot the difference. Consider first how well your own grander musical gestures align with those of the composer's, and indeed how close your instinct for the tempo turned out to be, before turning your attention to the finer intricacies.[103] You may find that your overall estimation of the music's intensity fits in rather plausibly with the composer's; where this appears to be not the case, see if you can reconcile the main differences and reach a compromise that works well in a practical way. You may also discover that you have rather more details in your organic score than are present in the original. This may be because the composer was content to confer much of the interpreting to you, the mindful pianist, or it may have more to do with historical precedents of performance practice.[104]

Here are two examples of organic scores for you to study before you create some of your own.

---

102 If you invite other people to contribute to your version, it will become effectively an 'edition by committee'.

103 A limitation of the 'organic score' approach is that important style-specific markings, implications or idiosyncrasies, such as Beethoven's *sforzando* and *subito piano* effects, are likely to pass undetected (unless one is specifically searching for them). Nevertheless, when making a final comparison with the printed score, the true impact of such features can be even more effectively realised.

104 We would not expect to find much by way of interpretive assistance in a 'clean' urtext of Bach's '48' by Henle for example, or Kenneth Gilbert's 'Le Pupitre' edition of Scarlatti's Sonatas, other than scholarly observations included in editorial commentaries. However, a dearth of markings should not be taken as evidence that the modern pianist must abstain from adding expressive variants. This is especially the case in places where the musical implications 'seem' overwhelmingly clear to us: my instinct has always been that the absence of proof is not the proof of absence.

Scarlatti, Sonata in E Major K.380

Baroque keyboard music poses its own very specific set of challenges for the modern player, and this is why it is potentially just as advantageous to apply an 'organic score' approach to a work by Scarlatti as by Rachmaninov.

This exquisite 'processional' sonata is brimming with possibilities for a mindful approach. Even in the composer's time there would surely have been a range of speeds and approaches which could serve the music equally well, notwithstanding Scarlatti's marking, *Andante commodo*, and the $\frac{3}{4}$ time signature, which may conceivably be taken to imply a pace lying somewhere between a minuet and a waltz.[105] Its catchy 'bare fifths' rhythmic motif can either be taken as encouragement to sprint along in a quasi-percussive style (perhaps imagining some kind of cheery pageantry involving tambourines and the like), or at a rather more sedate, 'regal' pace suggestive of a serious mood. Ironically, the former approach may appear to nudge the music towards a 'Classical' vein, while the latter could conceivably render the piece somewhat more 'Romantic'. Though this is surely not an uncommon dilemma in interpreting Scarlatti, the Sonata K.380 seems to me to be among the composer's more ambiguous examples as regards intensity; the piece invites us to really think hard about what we wish the listener to gain from the experience of encountering our performance.[106]

A first glance at the second half of this typical binary form sonata reveals little to frighten the horses.[107] The trouble begins when we have to pin our colours to the mast as regards dynamics, articulation and even pedalling.[108] The annotations I have made were entirely spontaneous, at least at first, in the spirit I have been encouraging the reader to take, though others were added subsequently at the piano. The arrows forward and back indicate my preferences for tempo flexibility. My instinct was to emphasise Scarlatti's ingenious harmonic scheme in relation to its gradual build up in register, which culminates in a (nearly) four-octave span at beat two of bar 55: A♯3 to G6. As I look at it now, I am left feeling that my 'edition' looks exceedingly Romantic, though the extent to which this might map onto my own performance is of course an entirely different matter.[109]

---

105 A waltz is generally assumed to work best at around a tempo of MM 84–90 beats per minute, whereas a minuet is often considered to be effective played somewhat slower, at around MM 60–80. If the minuet (a 'social' dance) was among the more popular 18th century dances, then surely the waltz would be among the more favoured 19th century dances. Though Scarlatti would likely not have known of the latter, our 21st century ears most certainly accommodate the generally more upbeat pulse attributed to it.
106 Most of us, I feel confident, would prefer to hear a committed interpretation played at twice (or indeed half) our own ideal speed than to have to sit through a half-baked rendition in which the performer has chosen to let the music 'speak for itself'.
107 The home key of E major modulates to its dominant, B major, at the double-bar (bar 41). From here, the music begins its long homeward journey. A daring sequential development between bars 45 and 56 reaffirms the dominant key; hence, the eventual return to the tonic, E major, at bar 72, appears all the more eventful.
108 If we are not prepared to commit to an edition on paper, our willingness to create an 'edition in sound' seems improbable.
109 The potential to vary the approach at the repeats (in practice, many pianists opt to just play the first of these) certainly adds further fuel to our imagination as we set about interpreting this wonderful sonata. We may, on balance, prefer to hold our emotional instincts in check until making the repeat.

Scarlatti, Sonata in E Major K.380, bb.41–60: skeleton score

Scarlatti, Sonata in E Major K.380, bb.41-60: organic score

Chopin, Prelude No.7 in A Major Op.28

The delightful and impressively brief 16-bar Prelude in A, turns out to be a goldmine of musical intensity.[110] Compare the skeleton score given below with my organic score to catch a glimpse of the possibilities for a viable interpretation. The climax seems rather obviously to be positioned at bar 12,

---

110 The majestic, thickly-textured Prelude No. 20 in C Minor Op.28 is even shorter (on paper, though not necessarily in performance), weighing in at just 13 bars.

precisely three-quarters of the way through, corroborated by both Chopin's use of register and the build-up in density.[111] What we end up with is the archetypal Romantic piano piece, with its own colourful story to tell,[112] though telescoped to daringly miniature proportions.[113]

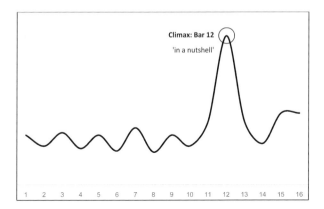

Chopin, Prelude No.7 in A Major Op. 28: skeleton score

111 An enraptured F♯ major chord (VI) marks the music's unmistakable emotional peak.
112 Alfred Cortot (1877–1962), was a Swiss-French pianist who famously created 'study scores' of all Chopin's piano music to go with his recordings. These editions are daringly replete with pedalling suggestions, phrasing and so on. Cortot also enjoyed adding his own emotional subtitles/nicknames to the Preludes, such as 'Homesickness' (No.6 in B minor) and 'Blood, Passion and Death' (No.24 in D minor). Incidentally, Cortot's recordings in the 1920s (among the earliest 'electric' recordings ever made), are a pure delight to listen to. His poetic style, not to everyone's taste to be sure, places him securely within a category of pianist at the time known as 'Chopinist'.
113 The graph depicting intensity is another idealisation, constructed in similar fashion to the Rachmaninov model described earlier. It takes account of Chopin's use of register and density (note *not* dynamics, for Chopin provides none aside from the opening *piano* and a small *crescendo* in bar 11), amalgamated into one compelling contour.

Chopin, Prelude No.7 in A Major Op. 28: organic score

Chopin, Prelude No.7 in A Major Op. 28: original score

9 The playfulness of playing

Serendipity

Have you ever stopped to consider the chain of events which led to a recent successful performance you gave? Now that you can play the piece well, it probably seems unconscionable that things could have turned out differently. And yet, along the way, there were probably times when you doubted your ability to reel off that knotty passage near the coda, or to memorise the complex harmonic scheme in the development section. The truth is that at each stage in the learning process serendipity almost certainly played a part in how things eventually turned out. A chance fingering, stumbled across early on, shaped the way you tackled umpteen subsequent passages. What started as an impossible cascade of notes on page three turned out to be your favourite part of the piece, but only because of an insightful remark nonchalantly gifted to you over the phone by a friend who had performed the piece the year before. All of these happenstance occurrences were 'lucky' in the sense that they might not have happened at all, or stimulated such a positive response in you, and yet your good fortune was actually only made possible by dint of your own endeavours. In other words, you created the environment in which your own good fortune could bear fruit.

Being alive to the possibilities of chance discoveries when practising is all part of being mindful.[114] We can only delight in moments of randomness if we are willing to acknowledge them as they crop up naturally, keeping some, dismissing others. A recurring theme of the book is that piano practice tends to be packed with events that distract us from the 'here and now'. Piano playing is a continual juggling act, so that enjoying spontaneity and exercising restraint often seem to work in opposing directions. We need to strike with purpose and have a robust end goal in sight, and yet we also need to feel free to embrace unsolicited ideas as they drip-feed unexpectedly during the practice process, for they may turn out to be momentous. Our capacity for playfulness should be treasured at least as greatly as our desire to play with sophistication.

Interestingly, we call what we do, piano *playing*, not piano *working*. I have tended to interchange 'playing' and 'working' in this book to fit the particular purpose I had in mind, without apology, and perhaps this is how best to think of it. When we are practising we are getting to grips with the nitty-gritty, pulling things apart and reuniting them, getting the ideas firmly into our heads and aiming to establish patterns of behaviour which will stand us in good stead. Like the golfer hoping to evolve a repeatable, dependable swing, we are paving the way for an, as yet, possibly 'un-experienced' act. We instinctively know when we are inching in the right direction, for at last the sections seem to knit together more fluidly, or are at least less fragmented. When we dare to

114 Performing is a pianist's opportunity to be a little different, to make one's mark.

consider what is coming up on the next page, such thoughts start to have a beneficial impact on the bar we are dealing with right now, instead of tripping us up, as they once did. Our playing will then have arrived at an altogether different domain in which we push our ideas forward and resist the temptation to backpedal. The syntax of the music, at least as we have come to understand it, is intact. Just as the golfer cannot 'play' golf (and arguably, derive much enjoyment from trying) until a rudimentary level of competence has been reached, the pianist cannot really play a piece until some level of continuity and progression of ideas is in place. First we work, *then* we play.

I think this is where the questionable notion of having 'fun' in our learning (of anything, not just piano playing) may have stemmed from, perhaps particularly in the past twenty years or so. We can be gaining *satisfaction* in our learning of a piano piece for many weeks, or even years, and yet may never feel inclined to describe the experience as fun.[115] As I hinted at the start of the book, if we are not gaining something of value from all of our picking and unpicking, why on earth are we doing it at all?

> It is important to be able to distinguish between practising and *practising performing*. For instance, when getting closer to giving a performance, consider returning to a much earlier stage of practice, such as slowly playing the last bar (or lines) of a piece, then the last two bars (or lines), then the last three bars (or lines) and so on. Finally, a single attempt to perform the whole piece at the end of the practice session, with a feeling that the preceding practise is building up to this, can be informative. By being disciplined about these two, clearly defined modes of work, the blurred division between 'half-practice' and 'half-performance' can be avoided. **Frederick Stocken**

There can surely be fewer skills more important for the novice pianist to learn than that of practising how to practise. Thought of in this way, a piano lesson presents an invaluable opportunity for the pupil to road-test some of the coming week's practice objectives.

The mindful collaborator

> For the pianist, who spends so much time in isolation (and there is nothing like the loneliness that can descend as you sit down at the piano on a concert platform), the joy of sharing the music-making with a singer or instrumentalist is beyond compare. Whether it be playing the accompaniment to the simplest song, or embarking on the journey that is a work like Schubert's *Winterreise* (or one of his Piano Trios) the inner satisfaction cannot be measured. Sharing helps you to forget yourself and allows you to become entirely wrapped up in the music.
> Margaret Murray-McLeod

115 If anyone tells me they are having 'fun' when playing Webern's *Variations*, I shall not be accepting an invitation to their next Christmas party. As an aside, I very much enjoyed Alfred Brendel's quip (in his recent book *Music, Sense and Nonsense*, Robson Press, 2015, p.85) that 'Humoresques are notoriously unfunny'.

Sharing, by its very definition, is an act of generosity. And yet generosity functions antithetically from much of what pianists typically engage in. One might say that the act of practising the piano is intrinsically selfish anyway – nobody but the pianist is present and nobody but the pianist is gaining any direct benefit. For many student pianists the very notion of spending time learning the piano part to, say, Franck's Violin Sonata, when they could be girding their loins with Beethoven's *Appassionata*, would seem preposterous.[116] For this reason, student pianists tend to hibernate and only emerge rubbing their eyes from the darkness in the late Spring, lured out by the slightly better weather and when the end of year recital assessment begins to loom large on the horizon. Hence the more capable and reliable pianists in any conservatoire or university year group will inevitably be festooned with admiring bribe-bearers around May or June, all wanting the services of a good, solid accompanist who turns up to rehearsals sober, on time, and who actually listens.

Historically, a good number of the abler pianists passing through higher music education seem disinclined to take up the challenge of accompanying on anything other than a token level. That said, there are some excellent specialist accompanying courses to be sought out; it would certainly make sense for more of these to sprout up in future, given that there will always be a greater amount of work for competent accompanists, répétiteurs, pit-band keyboardists and chamber players within the profession than for pianists who can romp through Rachmaninov's Second Piano Concerto. The solo pianist so quickly becomes proprietorial with practice time, and not without good reason, for even at college they can already feel the burden of a million heavyweight piano pieces bearing down on them from a great height.

Good soloists surprisingly rarely make comparably good accompanists (or more correctly, in the case of the aforementioned Franck, 'duo partners'), and this may have as much to do with time constraints as a reluctance to reach artistic decisions in partnership with someone else. Granted, being flexible enough to make musical connections with a fellow musician presupposes a level of technical acquisition and artistic insight which is not always going to be present in a student pianist.

Communicating as a soloist in any case turns out to be a wholly different matter from communicating while someone else is sharing your limelight. Knowing when to tuck yourself away (even though you rather like playing a particular passage because you know you can do it well) takes a level of maturity and understanding, which we cannot simply take for granted. But in truth, at least as much musical satisfaction can come from playing with others as when we are cocooned in a little room on our own. The trouble with a soloist's life is that it becomes increasingly difficult to accommodate other people's opinions – the act of interpreting, as I have been suggesting throughout, is vested on being

---

116 The truth is that it will likely take a diploma level pianist at least as long to learn the piano part to Beethoven's *Spring Sonata* as it would to learn one of the early period solo sonatas by the same composer.

decisive, after all – but this is why getting involved with other musicians can be so tremendously rewarding; it serves to recalibrate us and straighten out our motivations for playing the instrument.

> In my teaching I have enjoyed working with all manner of ensembles (six or eight hands on one piano, and eight, 12 and 16 hands on two pianos), as well as more conventional chamber music. This type of work improves the sight-reading – this might not immediately be obvious to the students themselves, though the need to listen and blend in with others, skipping beats if someone has omitted a bar perhaps, does eventually feed into the reading skills. Another aspect is rhythm – for if one student miscounts, the others must adapt in an instant. In ensembles of this type, concerts seem far less nerve-wracking, too – many players find it more fun to play with friends than all alone. Individual practice for the members of these ensembles is of course vital but, once done, the pleasure is immeasurable as students endeavour to blend together musically. Even those of my students who have contemplated quitting piano lessons have been successfully deterred, simply because of the fun and sense of involvement they gained from playing in an annual ensemble concert. In my experience during the last twenty years, progress is always made when enjoyment is at the heart of practice and performance. **Nadia Lasserson**

The 'problem shared' fringe-benefit of accompanying or playing in chamber groups for some pianists turns out to be rather crucial; we do not all have the resolve to be soloists on stage, even if we have a certificate on our wall which testifies to our having qualified as one.[117] Learning to work confidently and empathetically with others actually helps us to 'accompany ourselves' more poetically too, so if for no reason other than this we should take the bribe and learn the Franck *Sonata* – and *Winterreise*, for that matter. When we finally crawl back to our practice room and resume battle with the *Emperor Concerto*, we will undoubtedly be all the wiser and all the more convincing as we reel off those arpeggios.

Period instruments

Pianists need to be mindful of the instruments of the day, at least to a degree, and aware of the priorities with which performers from the Baroque and Classical eras might have tackled the music.[118] Even a scanty understanding of period instruments can provide invaluable insight into what fits best as regards a musical work's ever-changing texture for example, or what might constitute its optimum working tempo.[119] We should also open our minds to

---

117 Buck, P., 1944: *Psychology for Musicians* (Oxford, OUP).
118 I would encourage all pianists to read this seminal book: Sadie, S. and Brown H.M., 1990: *Performance Practice: Music after 1600* (New York, Norton). The author cuts to the chase as regards those aspects of performance practice pianists need to know about.
119 On instruments possessing a rapid decay, which includes the fortepiano as well as the harpsichord and clavichord, slow-moving music may well have been played faster than is generally the case today on the modern piano. Furthermore, the humble trill (which is really just an appoggiatura repeated a number of times, end on end) proved to be highly prized in the 18th century as a device for 'sustaining' important notes, especially at cadences.

how, why and where ornaments are likely to be helpful, even if not marked in.[120] Practical solutions to the conundrum of non-notated 'implied' dynamic effects, alongside *tenuto* notes and tempo *rubato*, all need to reflect, not mimic, what was once achievable by performers.

Although today we will often be faced with an instrument boasting three (or more) pedals,[121] we may actually be tackling a piece of music conceived for an instrument possessing none, such as the aforementioned Baroque keyboards.[122] Furthermore, we may be gearing up to play a full-sized grand in a large auditorium with an opulent echo, which could hardly contrast more with the softly-spoken instrument and diminutive performance space more typical of the 18th century.[123]

A few further points to keep in mind when playing 18th-century keyboard music on a modern piano:

- Scale down dynamics, but do not omit them. 'Terraced' dynamics are by no means the only weapon in the modern player's armoury; contemplate subtle gradations to help point up peaks of phrase, and be bolder when introducing voices in contrapuntal music. Projection of important lines, especially in larger performing spaces, is imperative if the listener is to savour your stylish ideas.

- Avoid 'woodpecker' syndrome (overly pecked *staccato* notes) and the dreaded 'sausage machine' (streams of shapeless, directionless notes) at all costs. Always be imaginative, resourceful and colourful; never an apologist of the piano.

- *Rubato*, contrary to popular opinion, is by no means solely the province of repertoire from the 19th century onwards, as a glance through Richard Hudson's enterprising book amply illustrates.[124] Carefully cited subtle tenuto effects can be artistic and poignant, even in faster-moving Baroque keyboard music.

- More often than not, tease out the 'moving parts' of the texture, which may of course arise in the left hand (Baroque and Classical composers often keep one part on the move, while the concurrent parts are given longer time-values).

- Pedal, though requiring restraint and 'virtuoso listening skills' at all times, is emphatically not a no-go area for pianists. Deft touches here and there, and even half-pedalling, can add a welcome frisson of personality.

---

120 Ornaments needed on a period instrument will not necessarily be imperative (or indeed practicable) on the piano; conversely of course, we may today feel encouraged to add certain embellishments at will. However, we might bear in mind CPE Bach's cautionary observation, 'ornaments are like spices that can ruin the best dish'. Bach, C.P.E., [1753, 1762] 1949: *Essay on the True Art of Playing Keyboard Instruments*, Trans. Mitchell, W.J. (New York, Norton).

121 The Fazioli F308 grand has no fewer than four pedals: sustain, *sostenuto*, *una corda* and half-blow (positioned to the left). Incidentally, this continues to be the instrument of choice for Bach specialist, Angela Hewitt.

122 The generic term for keyboards being 'clavier'. Some fortepianos did of course have a knee-operated sustain pedal, yet its functionality can hardly be compared to the foot-operated modern equivalent; judged by our 21st century ears, it was either 'on', or 'off'.

123 Bach's clavichord was so quiet that reportedly he could practise at one end of a church while a service was taking place at the other.

124 Hudson, R. 1997, *Stolen Time: The History of Tempo Rubato* (USA, Oxford University Press)

For me, clarity is the keyword when playing the music of Mozart. To convey the crystal textures of his piano works the performer must approach the very opening of each piece with care and precision. Not only chords, but individual notes, must be carefully voiced. Pedal should be applied sparingly – much of Mozart's music can be successfully interpreted with no pedal at all, though its thoughtful application can add magical moments of colour. Although unstylish *rubato* is to be avoided, passage-work should be given shape and not be 'rattled off', like a Czerny study. Neat, clean finger-work helps overcome the problem of playing fortepiano music on a pianoforte, but that, in itself, is not enough. The challenge is to add the emotional content without creating unnatural distortion. **Allan Schiller**

10 Exams: a view from the examiner's chair

I would like to offer some entirely personal ruminations from the 'other side' – the examiner's chair. There are no trade secrets or anything controversial here, but hopefully a few illuminating ideas as you gather yourself up to take your next graded piano exam, prepare your candidates or help your child in the lead up to an exam day. Mindfulness in the practice room is one thing, but mindfulness in an exam is something altogether more challenging.

The fact that piano exams 'matter' should not mean they matter more than other focal points in our musical lives, such as school concerts or piano club get-togethers. Exams are convenient markers along a continuum, but they are still performance situations, and like any performance there will always be a sense of the unknown to deal with. The possibility for something memorably beautiful to occur must always be tinged with the potential for small-scale calamities. Our biggest challenge is how to deal with the peculiarities of our own temperament. For most of us, the question is not whether we may encounter aspects of our playing which displease us on the day, but when, how and to what extent we will allow these things to get the better of us. Once exam candidates have a little experience under their belt, they usually start to realise that the compromises imposed by an unusual environment do not need to be unduly intimidating or undermining. Candidates usually learn to calm themselves in response to the positive experience they had last time with that rather nice examiner wearing the orange tie.

> Exams provide goals, motivation and important measures of success from recognised bodies. They can provide the main motivation for mastering scales or sight-reading, for example, and this can lead to a satisfying sense of achievement. But we need to use exams wisely, recognising how they do, and do not, help us progress. If our ideal is to be able to play inspiring music spontaneously, by ear and using improvisation – not just by reading notes – we need to seek out syllabuses which encourage this, and look carefully at the repertoire to be sure such things are being actively encouraged.[125]
> Lucinda Mackworth-Young

For the more senior candidate, keeping exams in perspective may be easier said than done. The attitude of mind we have during the run up to an exam is therefore critical to the approach we end up taking as we stroll into the room. When things go a little astray, rehearse how you hope to react – can you keep your neuroses at bay and hold your nerve? One poorly-executed scale need not cause you to crash in all the others.

---

125 Although the importance of improvisation is rarely denied in prominent educational circles, alas, it continues to play only the tiniest role within the suite of piano examinations offered by the foremost boards (ABRSM Jazz and Practical Musicianship Syllabuses, TCL Supporting Tests).

We need to come to terms with the fact that, unlike a maths exam, we will not be encouraged to go back over mistakes and 'fix' them – the mental Tippex we permit ourselves at home is perhaps among the hardest things to leave behind us as we sit down to take an exam. Hence, we should wherever possible approach exams just as we would a 'public' performance – excited at what we have inside us, ready to share with others, but tempered with an awareness of the imperfectness the situation inevitably poses.

It takes practice and forethought to become an efficient taker of exams. This is true irrespective of the subject. Paradoxically, as we grow older, the level of adrenaline-fuelled anxiety, even when playing for an audience of one, can seem inordinately great unless steps are taken to prepare for the rather specific set of circumstances likely to be encountered.[126] Many youngsters seem able to breeze in and enjoy their piano exam free from the burden of thinking the outcome is going to be a game-changer for the rest of their lives.[127] They have not 'learned' what nerves are, and lucky are they, because despite parents' and teachers' best intentions, exam candidates can have a tendency over time to become increasingly aware of what the exam 'is'.

Adults would be best advised to keep the exam experience as low-key and light-hearted as they can for their young people, since their own anxieties and sense of the exam's importance can inadvertently lead to a ramping up of tension. Without realising it, the earnest adult brings their own baggage and personal history to bear. The more a child is reminded that the 'dreaded' exam is looming, the more they may take on the angst of their parents, who might not have grasped the fact that the true benefit of a piano exam lies in the weeks and months leading up to it. We can choose whether to think of the exam as an opportunity to play a beautiful, newly-tuned piano in front of someone with a fresh perspective to offer, or to imagine it to be an ordeal, like going to the dentist. An entourage of well-meaning parents, siblings and pets in the exam waiting room is the worst possible way of helping to keep this sense of perspective. Though examiners are experienced in the subtle craft of nerve-management, we are not miracle-workers or trained councillors; we may not be able to mollify in seconds the child who has been wound up like a spring since seven o'clock that morning.

The consequences of not doing well in an exam are hardly likely to be significant in the long-run, and teachers, for the most part, know that success is entirely contextual – for some players a Distinction is on the cards, while for others a Pass will constitute a significant and praiseworthy achievement. Teachers also know that the only person worth comparing yourself with is *yourself* – how you progress in relation to your own industry and experience. But all too easily the ambitions of parents, and occasionally teachers too, trickle into the vulnerable minds of youngsters.

126 One of my summer school students once confided in me that he gets nervous playing scales, even at home, and they become even worse when his cat strolls into the room – he meant it, too. (I recommended that the cat took up permanent residence in his music room, or that he puts earmuffs on his cat so that it would not judge him so harshly).
127 It is very important for exam candidates (regardless of age) to leave behind any notion that there is only the one chance to succeed.

Different approaches

I am continually startled by the approaches taken by candidates as they walk in, meet my eyes and sit down in readiness to play. Some manage to start their first piece even before their backside has reached the chair, while others prefer the Ivo Pogorelich approach – they saunter into the room, shimmy up to the stool, assess it, grimace, sit down, offer a hand up to the keyboard but recoil as though a rattle snake has just appeared from under the lid, sigh, and finally place the book on the stand.

There is no right or wrong approach to taking an exam, but it is sometimes the case that the candidate appears to be hindered by their own desire to do well, or in some cases perhaps weighed down by perceived shortcomings. Very occasionally, I have found myself feeling fractionally unnerved by a candidate's breathless determination. As they charge manically through their pieces I notice I am writing faster and faster, as though there is some kind of race under way. Alas, the impulse to scurry through scales and pieces at top speed as a symptom of uncontrolled nerves, will often undermine the quality of what is presented.

This paints the worst conceivable extreme, and is by no means something examiners are challenged by routinely, but even in less striking cases it calls to question an approach which has backfired for the candidate, whose playing cannot have been able to shine as it otherwise may have done. A great deal can be done to head off this potentially debilitating scenario by framing the exam as something to be cherished and looked forward to, a chance to make music and really 'wow' the examiner. Much hinges on an ability to monitor the child's progress from arm's length, not too fervently or with too many suggestions, prompts and knee-jerk reactions just before the exam day. We often call it the 'big' day, but it is perhaps more fruitful to think of it as the 'special' day.

The exam will inevitably flow along more swiftly than a typical lesson, or even a full run-through. By experiencing one or two mock exams in the weeks prior to the exam, the candidate can begin to sense the fluid movement between items and should not feel surprised at how their time in the exam room plays itself out. The exam is a time to enjoy performing and to demonstrate 'ownership' of the music. This applies as much to the individual items within the supporting tests as the pieces themselves. We should be encouraged to rehearse how to breathe, calm ourselves and take stock of what is happening as we come to take an exam.[128]

For some instrumentalists a new performing space can be slightly distracting, but at least the instrument itself will be an old friend. The pianist however

---

128 Teachers frequently like to annotate their pupils' scores. The tradition for doing this is long and well-documented. We know a significant amount about Chopin's own playing and teaching methods from the markings he made in scores owned by his pupils, notably Jane Sterling (1804–1859). See Eigeldinger, J-J, 1991: *Chopin: Pianist and Teacher* (Cambridge, Cambridge University Press). Done judiciously, this is certainly to be recommended; however, annotating can turn into something of an obsession. Some of the scores I have spotted languishing in exam rooms contain more highlighted markings and crossings-out than the original printed text; in such cases the pupil (not to mention the teacher) may well have lost the ability to see the wood for the trees.

must usually contend with an unfamiliar instrument too, which may look as different from the piano at home as a Lamborghini parked next to a Smart Car. A heavier touch may also be apparent, and it would be a good idea to seek out opportunities to practise on different 'bigger' instruments if possible, to head off the shock of encountering a grand piano for the first time, or indeed a brighter upright. Children especially need to imagine that the sound might be considerably louder – they should be encouraged not to fight it, but go with it in pursuit of an assertive, impactful performance, rather than 'tickle' the keys in the hope of keeping the noise down. Good piano playing in a small room will inevitably sound loud, and this takes some getting used to.

Should I play from memory?

Playing from memory sometimes proves to be the piano candidate's *bête noire*. In some cases, the candidate unfortunately ends up demonstrating what they cannot yet do, as opposed to what they had hoped they might. It is not uncommon for pianists to 'know' the music better than they know how to *play* it. The potential benefits of playing without the score are not infrequently outweighed by the insecurities and breakdowns that inadvertently arise, and the 'half-memorised' state is surely the most precarious of all. It is my experience that amateur pianists tend to prize memorising too highly, possibly as a response to what they presume to be a hallmark of professionalism. The newness of the surroundings, and the mere presence of an examiner, can tug the pianist's attention away from the music in ways not hitherto encountered, so careful thought needs to be given to the question of whether or not to memorise. Learning, of course, is memorising, at least to an extent, which is why we are able to play complex music fluently with a score (when on first encountering it we could only stumble through). There are very few piano exams which decree the need to memorise, though it is often expected at conservatoire level, where of course an entirely different set of ambitions have been set in motion and the player is that bit closer to emulating the performance practices of a professional player.

Many young pianists learn their pieces and scales by a combination of rote and reading, which presents a subtly different range of scenarios as regards playing from memory in the exam. It is not uncommon to see a candidate place the book open to their first piece and never look at it again – once finished, they flip over the page and proceed to do the same thing with pieces two and three. Should something go awry, the candidate will struggle to relocate themselves, and worse still, may feel the need to start again from the top. It is also worth weighing up the extent to which the musically important details of the pieces have been thoroughly memorised (as opposed to merely the notes and rhythms) – for it is with these details that a candidate can really have something to say.

Keeping a sense of perspective

Exam candidates need to be encouraged to treat their piano exam as just another increment in their learning – a point on the road of progress as opposed to journey's end. They are more likely to coax out a quiet smile from the examiner if they are at ease with what they are doing, which of course is predicated upon the approach taken by themselves, their parents and teacher from months earlier. They should be encouraged to 'share' their scales, not rattle them off, and to play each item with a calm sense of engagement, rather than seek to impress with velocity, reckless feats of memory or sheer volume. One could even consider 'ghosting' one or two trickier scale items prior to launching in head-first, just to be clear about the patterns. Rehearsing the first few bars in one's head before the start of each piece (and indeed the sight-reading) is a time-honoured way of ensuring a realistic speed, as well as homing in more immediately on the musical character.[129]

Doing well in a piano exam is not a 'trick', despite my earlier point about garnering valuable experience over time. It is more about allowing things to happen at an unhurried pace, with the integrity of the music kept higher up in the priorities than any notions of success or failure. It is important to gain an ability to recover from the initial surprise of hearing yourself play a ghastly, conspicuous wrong note, and to allow it to simply pass. All is not lost when little things go wrong – or even one or two big things, necessarily – for unlike a driving test there is no calamitous equivalent of hitting the curb in a piano exam.[130]

The last thing that should be on the candidate's mind is the total number that will eventually appear on the mark form. Though from the candidate's perspective the exam experience may feel somewhat subjective and encumbered by moments of unexpected turbulence, it is worth remembering that the examiner is taking an objective view – what was actually heard – and nothing else. The examiner is not interested in whether a candidate has been working at the pieces for two years or two weeks, merely what impact they have on the day. The 'real' musician is often far more in evidence than the candidate fears is the case as they scrabble around in the scale of D♭ major or realise too late that they overlooked the $\frac{6}{8}$ time-signature in the sight-reading. Examiners have an antenna for the qualities of musicianship that each candidate possesses. A candidate's willingness to learn from the experience – and from the examiner's comments – not merely to celebrate or commiserate the result a few weeks later, is a key component in the exam's intrinsic worth. The parent and teacher have important roles to play in helping to keep this sense of perspective so that the exam becomes something to be anticipated with a smile the next time around.

Speaking of keeping things in perspective, it is worth observing that man cannot live by exams alone. The race to the finishing line of grade 8 may in some cases be

---

129 Golfers are often trained to have a 'swing-thought' – a single conception to help them execute their next shot.
130 An escalation of smaller troublesome events, which could cause a candidate to tighten up and progressively lose control, might however become a different matter.

seen as a hollow victory. To my knowledge, no exam board ever gave extra credit for attaining the highest grade by a certain age. If a pianist has only clocked up a total of 24 pieces in their playing history (i.e. three for each grade), then one might well question the overarching learning philosophy. It is worth keeping in mind that while exam boards provide a convenient mechanism for advancement, the task of consolidation invariably comes down to the teacher. The breathing space which should ideally intervene before embarking upon the next exam is surely as important as the months the student may take in preparation for it. Besides, arguably it is good to have something still to work towards.

The vulnerability exam candidates occasionally feel is not just inevitable, it is invaluable in building a sense of who they are as human beings and coming to terms with the wonderful challenges and unpredictability of life. Without it, they cannot hope to 'spend' what they have learned about their own musical personalities. This is why a piano exam can be such an enlightening experience, for candidates get to discover aspects of themselves they might not otherwise. When a young pianist first experiences what it is to rise above momentary aberrations and access their raw instincts as a creative musician, a significant milestone has been reached. From here, the direction of travel can become even more positive, energetic and likely to filter into other aspects of his/her life.

> As an examiner of written, composing and performance exams, I am made aware every time a script, piece or performer appears before me for assessment, that I am not only judging their technical and expressive prowess, but their very inner self. Each decision made in practice, each thought formed in revision and each marking made on the score, is the result of some degree of mindfulness and integrity of that living, breathing human being. The greatest joy is seeing and hearing a creation of any sort, shaped by careful and caring thought, even if the underlying technique might otherwise appear lacking. **Gillian Poznansky**

Afterthoughts for teachers

The teacher's priorities almost invariably become the pupil's priorities. Examiners sometimes feel this palpably if, upon later reflection, certain attributes seem to have been seeping through into several candidates' performances. If the teacher cares deeply about scales, for example, then it is more likely that a good number of their pupils will, too; ditto other aspects of learning. Physical traits spotted in a number of pupils from the same teacher may also have their roots in that teacher, for example peculiarities of posture, exaggerated body-swaying, grunting, loud sniffing, and singing while playing. Teachers of course want their best attributes to stick with their pupils; the downside is that not all copied mannerisms or habits will be helpful; every visual and aural detail of a teacher's characteristics has the potential to be picked up.[131]

---

131 Alas, our playing will never be any nearer to Radu Lupu's or Glenn Gould's simply by assuming their idiosyncratic sitting posture (Gould sat impossibly low, while Lupu looks as though he might fall off the back of his chair at any moment).

Perhaps the best way to ensure all important aspects of the 'rounded' musician become inculcated into pupils in their weekly piano lessons is to integrate them imaginatively and pro-actively. Paul Harris's *Simultaneous Learning*[132] approach chimes rather well with a philosophy many teachers may have tentatively explored over the years, though it is unquestionably of great value to be shown how to build steadily and progressively from the known to the unknown, ensuring measurable achievement is always the outcome. One might reflect that simultaneous learning becomes all the more practicable when 'simultaneous teaching' has become thoroughly and instinctively embraced. The point is, teachers can either preoccupy themselves with attempting to sift out those things which have been insecurely learned (i.e. moving in reverse), or spend their time more profitably by building up patiently (i.e. moving forwards). Theoretical aspects are usually best taught on a 'need-to-know' basis; after all, we learn to speak far earlier than we learn to write. A steady trickle of carefully-posited facts will likely lodge themselves more readily in the pupil's memory than a blizzard of bamboozling details. Indeed, pupils tend to respond better when the teacher is able to be really clear in laying out objectives, offering perhaps just one or two important take-home messages for each piece.

It is not uncommon to encounter candidates whose overall result does not fully reflect their *playing* ability. Where good marks in the pieces are not backed up elsewhere, unfortunately the supporting tests are not so much a support as a hindrance. For those looking to take their playing to the next level – conservatoire or university perhaps – this can be frustrating, especially since it is in these areas that conscientious attention to an exam board's requirements can pay impressive dividends.

While many piano teachers consider exams to play an indispensable role (for they offer a readymade structure for teaching the instrument effectively, quite apart from what their pupils can get out of them), it seems only a small number invest regularly in their own wellbeing. This is hugely important, both for maintaining morale and keeping up to date. Teaching courses, such as EPTA UK's excellent Piano Teachers' Course, are one way of recharging the batteries, alongside summer schools, but so are taking qualifications: why not enrol on an external graduate or master's degree course (there are part-time options aplenty these days).[133] Working towards a teaching diploma can be a tremendously revitalising pursuit too, as it will inevitably unearth myriad modern ways of thinking about age-old problems and bring you into contact with other like-minded teachers.[134] Reconsidering repertoire is another potential eye-opener for the more established teacher, who may otherwise find themselves revolving around the same tutor books and favoured anthologies year on year, perhaps lacking the confidence to explore the staggering mass of new material added to every month. In my experience,

---

132 Harris, P., 2014: *Simultaneous Learning* (London, Faber).
133 www.pianoteacherscourse.org
134 ABRSM's Dip.ABRSM, LRSM and FRSM, and Trinity College London's ATCL, LTCL and FTCL all have options for teaching.

those who continually nourish themselves as 'mindful teachers' smile longest. Moreover, their obvious enjoyment of what they are doing spills over palpably to pupils, who invariably find the enthusiasm and sheer drive of a cheerful, dynamic teacher utterly irresistible.

Part 4

Engaging

11 Learning how we learn

Keeping masterclasses in perspective

It can sometimes be hard to make sense of apparently conflicting views regarding our playing in the masterclass setting. I have experienced this myself a number of times, and it can be quite testing of one's resilience and independence – 'X thinks I am playing it too fast, but Y recommends it goes even faster' etc. Often this simply comes down to a question of subtly different emphases or priorities, not 'contradictory' advice as such. Indeed, within these pages, by now the reader will doubtless have noticed occasional differences of opinion among the various contributors; these merely serve to widen our awareness of the possibilities. We may, for example, have been encouraged to slow down our playing under the guidance of our regular teacher, perhaps because s/he has reason to reign us in, whereas in the masterclass scenario the 'maestro' could well have an entirely different agenda – to bring us out of ourselves, or to encourage a better sense of line. At other times, we perhaps learn more about the bee in the bonnet of the advice-giver than intrinsic shortcomings in our own playing.

Nobody knows more about your body than you; think carefully before making wholesale changes to an approach which you feel is working acceptably well. A trumpeter friend was told in a masterclass that he needed to completely rethink his embouchure if he wanted to stand any chance of taking up a professional career. Against his better instincts, he followed the advice and ruined his playing for quite some time; eventually, he reverted to what he had originally been doing and successfully recaptured his ambition to play in a professional orchestra.

Our pragmatism as pianists ought not to dissuade us from prizing our own musical intelligence as highly as in others; nor should we lose our willingness to inch away from our comfort-zone from time to time. Ultimately though, we need to toughen up if we are going to lay ourselves bare in a masterclass situation, as anyone who has watched the infamous Paul Tortelier cello masterclasses will doubtless have discovered for themselves.[135] We should be willing to learn from different teachers, but this will only be possible if we are able to keep an open mind and refrain from too much internal debate afterwards. A pinch of salt here and there can make the difference between a positive and negative experience. Take on board the good advice and cheerfully bin the rest.

---

135 Paul Tortelier (1914–1990), French cellist, conductor and composer, who (briefly) taught Jacqueline du Pré at the Paris Conservatoire. His televised masterclasses of the 1970s go down as among the most memorable and enlightening ever documented. A critic once said of Tortelier, 'if Casals is Jupiter, then Tortelier is Apollo'.

The rise of the independent learner

We learn the piano very differently from how we once did. A century ago one might imagine fledgling pianists being brought up exclusively on a diet of serious 'Classical' repertoire, punctuated at regular intervals by studies designed to further harness a young pianist's technical and musical resources.[136] These days, by stark contrast, we seem awash with YouTube channels inviting players to tackle every conceivable element of learning. We now have a vast array of excellent digital resources to work with too,[137] and these successfully augment the hard-copy literature handed down to us from the pedagogues from yesteryear. Some of us may even feel we now have all we need to propagate our passion for piano playing independently.

This progressive gear-shift in the learning process has culminated in a pithier, more hands-on approach than ever before: we can have a cartoon of Lang Lang playing and pointing things out for us right in our living rooms, if we are minded to. Perhaps inevitably however, the possibilities for learning important tangential musical topics, such as theory – the kinds of things teachers might feel inclined to 'drop in' in passing during a piano lesson – seem less easy to accommodate via the Internet. An online video, after all, provides not so much an interactive experience as an instructive aid. 'Inessential' topics either have to be skated over or served up as side-dishes for those who feel sufficiently intrigued to bother. The possibility for spontaneous discussion cannot exist in the way a real teacher would consider to be entirely normal.

On balance, the immediacy of the Internet has livened things up immeasurably. The sturdier examples of Internet-based piano learning – 'E-Music Maestro', to name but one[138] – take the learner through an impressively progressive set of stages, which become added to over time; we may dip in and out, play and replay, to our heart's content. Typically, these tackle many enjoyably relevant topics, the bulk of which will be highly familiar to your experienced piano teacher, and when used as part of the overall learning process can prove a terrifically powerful aid. We are free to garner as many 'tips and tricks' from like-minded amateurs and experts as we have the inclination and time to access, inexpensively too, sat at home with an iPad perched on the piano. However, as with anything else learned solely from the Internet, it comes down to us to sort the wheat from the chaff, and hence to work through all of the possibilities for ourselves as we keep our fingers crossed we are making the right choices. An increasing number of piano blogsites assist stoically in weighing all this up for us,[139] though we still need to know precisely what we are looking for, and all the while our precious practising time is whittling away.

---

136 The somewhat draconian notion of needing to sit like an aristocrat, with a bible under the armpit and a ruler on the forearm is, thankfully, obsolete.
137 ABRSM's 'Piano Practice Partner' would be an excellent example: www.abrsm.org
138 www.e-musicmaestro.com
139 'Cross-Eyed Pianist' is one good example: www.crosseyedpianist.com. An excellent YouTube channel, which includes interviews with top pianists and also provides practical playing tips, is by Melanie Spanswick: https://www.youtube.com > ClassicalMel

The learning experience has altered beyond description. Nevertheless, even though the avenues by which we might choose to learn the piano continue to splinter off in interesting directions, some things remain reassuringly constant. We should not be distracted from what it is that the teacher can offer: immediate feedback and tailor-made advice. Aside from Skype-style lessons and webinars (the latter being geared towards groups, not the individual),[140] our own specific needs end up being pushed into the long grass; a solely independent approach to learning the piano will likely have its pitfalls.

The teacher however, offers a traditional package, which places the pupil at its epicentre. Of course teachers have always called upon an array of generic approaches to such matters as teaching scales, aural and so on, but these approaches will inevitably be forced to diversify moment by moment to accommodate the idiosyncrasies present in each pupil. An all-purpose approach will take the teacher so far, but soon there will be a need to respond, refocus and re-strategise. Teaching is only teaching in the sense most of us understand it when this feedback process is able to function, and function well.

An encouraging upshot of all of this is that we now seem to be taking extra responsibility for our own learning process; we have moved away from the notion that having an able teacher is the only conceivable way forward, and have become willing to consider other valuable and interesting ways of making progress partly under our own steam. That said, the experienced piano teacher will always hold an inestimably important role in the serious pursuit of improvement; no amount of supplementary material will ever upstage the gently observant thoughts and insights of a qualified, imaginative teacher. Teachers bring their own enthusiasm, wit, opinions and energy to the learning process, the sum of which propels the learner forward in ways impossible to simulate on one's own through the Internet. A desert island approach will get us so far, but in all probability not very far.

---

140 A webinar is an abbreviation of 'web-based seminar', in which participants are invited to interact (either verbally or using desktop applications) via sophisticated video conferencing software. Hence, although continual 'feeding back' is a strong feature of webinars, there will almost inevitably be an overarching agenda. A webinar is, therefore, geared up not so much to address the individual's needs as the interests of the group as a whole.

12 All in the mind

The tension dimension

Tension in piano playing is perhaps best thought of as a (hopefully) temporary glitch, not a full-system malfunction. That said, a feeling of mild anguish or apprehension can all too easily corkscrew itself into a mania. If we do not possess the resources needed to fix an issue, we inadvertently elevate it to the level of unconquerable; our demons seem to know precisely what they need to grow into monsters.[141] Think how easily we turn a perfectly solid, stable performance into a white-knuckle ride, just by permitting it to scurry away fractionally too quickly in the heat of the moment. We instinctively understand the need to work through those aspects of a piece giving us difficulty, yet ironically it is the act of overthinking that incapacitates us and may even halt progress in its tracks. We will not resolve our anxieties by awarding them a status they do not deserve.

> If I ever feel uncomfortable, tense, stressed or 'on edge' in piano playing, then I focus on the pulse. In a performance situation especially, it is vital to sustain a firm rhythmic awareness and control. Discomfort, tension and stiffness can be overcome through rhythmic vibrancy, for *rhythm* is the life force of music. Its power affects every aspect of music-making and largely determines the character, structure and quality of every live performance. Rhythm can immediately and effectively be empowered through regular, strong and purposeful breath control. In addition, a robust, purposeful, comfortable and commanding posture at the instrument will encourage rhythmic authority. Kathryn Page

Tension starts in the mind and dribbles incipiently down into our bodies. Its effects creep up on us like a silent snake, tightening the neck muscles and constricting our back and limbs. We look down at our fingers and see the veins popping, tendons raised and wrists welded to our arms like a manikin in a shop window. We respond by repositioning ourselves badly at the piano and by adopting any number of compensatory movements – one shoulder is raised higher than the other, the feet have become crossed under the seat and the arms have started to splay outwards. Worse still, tension is not often experienced in isolation from other physical and mental ailments; quickly we become frustrated and short-tempered.[142]

It occurs to me that tension in piano playing is either a massive subject deserving of a dozen weighty tomes, or a preoccupation of our own construction, better shrugged off with a healthy dollop of benign neglect. As Philip Fowke sagely observes in his Foreword, we more than likely make the

---

141 It seems many pianists confuse musical intensity with physical tension.
142 If we sit slumped at the piano, neck drooped forward, elbows sagging downwards, our mood is likely to deteriorate further; conversely, adopting an upright posture, fit for purpose, can stimulate a more attentive, alert response to the music we are working on.

issue of tension worse by dwelling on it unduly. This is the law of unintended consequences, when in all probability the first – and quite possibly final step in overcoming tension once and for all – is quite simply to tell ourselves to relax.

> Tension in piano playing is not just concerned with arms and hands – healthy posture at the piano is imperative, too. Neck, back, shoulder and spine discomfort can be alleviated by being aware of and improving sitting posture, as well as hand, arm and finger technique. Moreover, when practising and teaching, I recommend pianists factor in short 'unwinding' intervals. Melvyn Cooper

Whatever tension is, it can certainly feel wearyingly real for pianists who suffer from it. Ultimately, tension just gets in our way; perhaps we should try ignoring it, for it might just go away.

The curse of perfectionism

It is always worth considering the following question as we set out to learn or relearn a piece: just how good does it need to be? This is not a facetious question or one designed to build in a let-out clause even before we have started. The answer surely reflects the end goal – is it to perform in a high-profile recital, to succeed in an exam, or perhaps simply to enrich our own personal grasp of a particular style, with no immediate performance outlet in mind?

Surely the answer to this question should be allowed to influence what happens next. Let us start with two extremes. A concert performance of a piece is (in most eventualities) the opposite of a sight-read through it – the former will require endless hours of thoughtful work, while the latter amounts to an immediate seat-of-the-pants experience in which there is hardly any time to learn from mistakes, let alone correct them. When we sight-read something tricky we expect there to be imprecisions galore – we shrug our shoulders and accept them with a smile, or at least partly, as we have come to recognise that a broad survey is not only acceptable but in many cases inevitable.

We do not permit ourselves this degree of largesse when we perform of course, and I am not suggesting we should. However, the time it takes to achieve an acceptably solid performance of a Mozart Sonata will for most of us be only a tiny percentage of the time it would take to achieve a recording or live performance of the same piece.[143] The choice becomes starkly simple: within a comparable timeframe we can either achieve partial success with a dozen sonatas or excellence with perhaps one or two. If we take account of the fact that leaving a piece for a few years can itself produce nothing short of miraculous results – the gestation period may itself have caused our playing to improve – then the trade-off between striving for perfection now or being patient and leaving a piece 'unfinished' is less cut and dried. If, on the other hand, we take the wholly opposite, indeed conventional, stance and insist on

---

143 It is not uncommon to encounter pianists whose sight-reading ability is excellent, but whose 'final' performances never seem to get appreciably better; any tendency to over-invest in certain areas seems likely to result in a deficit elsewhere.

regarding every putative performance as equally important, then we ignore the palpable truth of a life teeming with other priorities. Attention to detail amounts to so much more than tunnel-vision perfectionism; it should be about piercing the surface of the score and daring to inject into it our own confident personality.

A good solution to this is to make a mental note of the stage currently reached with the learning of any particular piece: 'busk', 'sight-read-plus', 'half-memorised', 'performable (apart from the coda)', 'in the bag', etc. As time is fixed, while our ambitions usually are not, we need to learn how to allocate our practising optimally. This may require us to leave some of our learning incomplete, unready for public consumption – perhaps forever.

If we can be compassionate with ourselves, accept this minor transgression and move on in our lives, we will have turned an important corner in determining our position in the musical world. Beethoven would surely have forgiven us for not reaching an apotheosis of performance in his piano sonatas – the question is, *can we?* Perhaps we have become so accustomed to thinking in terms of failure or success in learning pieces of music (I am thinking about exams and the other 'measurable' benchmarks) we cannot abide the thought of leaving unfinished business. But unless you happen to be John Lill,[144] the likelihood is that you will never have a vast library of concertos at your fingertips for a performance at the drop of a hat, so perhaps it would be better, on balance, to learn to live with this reality, rejoice in the two-and-a-half concertos you can play acceptably well, and resolve to be calm about it.

Cross-talk and mind-wandering

Despite my assertion earlier that we need to have ready access to the piano in our heads, there is a point beyond which too much 'head talk' and 'head play' just becomes a drain on our resources. We all know what it is like to have a soundtrack to our lives droning on in the background, and it is by no means always the case that this is unhelpful. Without it, we might miss out on useful prompters about the music we are performing ('here comes that pivot chord... now ease off before the Fugue'). But there is a malevolent side to our alter-egos, which doubts our ability to pull off the tricky passage coming up on the next page, or questions how elegantly we just dispatched that left-hand trill. We pass judgement on virtually everything we play a nanosecond after we have done it, and the more ambitious for success we are, the more inclined to be critical we are programmed to become. The cruelty we subject ourselves to is inordinately worse than the words others would dream of foisting upon us.

The good news is that we can, to some extent, mollify the voice of doubt and replace it with a more supportive, constructive persona. This is not about learning to lie to ourselves or give incorrect feedback, for such self-delusion is surely worse for us in the long run than any number of negative digs we

144 John Lill's concerto repertoire apparently stretches to beyond 70. Lill is a British pianist, born 1944, who performed Rachmaninov's Third Concerto aged 18 under Sir Adrian Boult.

are capable of inflicting upon ourselves. It is about learning to stand up to ourselves as we would if someone else uttered those same words to us.

Something I have used extensively over the years is a mental version of the 'elastic-band snap', whereby a person snaps the elastic band around their wrist every time they feel the urge to self-harm or self-deprecate. The momentary 'pain' this inflicts jolts them into a heightened sense of the present; hence they move swiftly from a potentially harmful scenario (such as lighting up another cigarette) into a more positive frame of mind. My own version of this makes a play of certain key words which I am able to summon in an instant; they are remarkably simple, but they work for me.

The first two words I use come in response to the unnerving 'out-of-body' sensation that I experience from time to time when I am performing – I am watching my fingers whizz around the keyboard, conscious that I am sat there playing, and yet it is as though I am watching someone else playing. I internally shout 'listen!', then 'breathe!', which causes me to do both things in a split second. This 'reality check' effectively 'snaps' me back into the moment, and reduces the distance I have allowed to occur between myself and the music. 'Listen!' brings the sentience of the music to me, like a dose of smelling salts, making me feel alert, while 'breathe!' reminds me to take on sufficient air to refuel my brain, because I usually find that a sense of temporary shock occurs as I shift my mind from a passive state to an active one.

Like any learned response, you will need to come up with your own 'snap' words to arrest the problem state you find yourself experiencing, and then set about practising it while at home on your own. 'Snap' words only work because they bring about a rehearsed reaction in you which you have grown to trust and rely upon. I find that when I am teaching I often resort to calling out words, such as 'relax!' when a pupil is visibly hunching over, or 'shoulders!', 'wrist!' if the tension manifests itself in a more specific way, and I suppose this is where I learned to use snap words to awaken myself when the need arises. When I call out certain words to a pupil, more often than not I spot an immediate, palpable improvement – more importantly, so does the pupil. They grow accustomed to the words I blurt out during the lesson, such as 'tempo!' to stop from hurrying, 'volume!' if the playing is getting overly loud, or 'pedal!' if the foot is getting lazy; I dare say these words gradually permeate into their own playing (I hope they do) so that pupils gradually become capable of summoning them for themselves.

Of central importance in such methods is the shift from the head back to the body. All physical movements start off as impulses in the brain – but we play the piano with our fingers, arms and feet – not with our heads. A concept is only a concept until it becomes a sound. The body can, in its renewed state of wakefulness, enter into a dialogue with the head and placate its tendency to finger-wag by the evidence of the beauty in the music itself. It is like being forced to eat some strange, exotic food, which we tell ourselves looks ghastly, but then allow our taste buds to feed back the unexpected truth that we rather enjoyed it. We can learn to be more open to the possibility that our body is a better advocate of what we are capable of than our head, which seems intent on supplanting its suspicions in a bid to outmanoeuvre us.

We are often not reliable reporters of facts when it comes to our piano playing. We exaggerate our failings, diminish our qualities and often take a cynical view of positive comments even when we are lucky enough to receive them. The voice in our head is not *us*, it is an unruly, frequently belligerent persona that happens to have taken up squatter's rights. Like a noisy lodger living in the attic, we need to learn to accept its presence and get on with our musical lives – we will never be able to eject it or snuff it out entirely, but we can certainly get better at understanding its motives and learn to retaliate assertively. Patience and mindfulness in the practice room is the key to lifting up the undeniable beauty of what we are doing, so that our spiteful alter-ego is forced to relent while we get on with playing the piano.

It's the thought that counts

Though you may feel driven to distraction (at times, literally), clutching onto one simple thought as you embark on a performance can be an effective way of re-establishing the vital connection between you and what you are doing. A teacher of mine suggested that one should simply reflect on the fact that no one in the audience is likely to be able to play as well as you – this works rather less reliably with an audience of peers, needless to say. It might be worth bearing in mind that audiences do not have collective intelligence. Each person sat there has a single pair of ears and will arrive at just one view; in all probability, ten percent may be mulling over options for supper, while a further ten percent appear more interested in your choice of socks, or the wasp that has delighted in dive-bombing the keyboard. Some performers like to imagine their audience is naked, sat on the loo, or having their ingrowing toenails removed; others fix their gaze on one perpetually smiling member of the audience sat quite far back. Mercifully, in most instances (including exams), pianists are faced 90-degrees from their audiences, so they are at least spared the issues facing a singer. I've given over 300 recitals on cruise ships around the world, and it is not uncommon for members of the audience to slope off mid-way through (or, more annoyingly, two notes into the penultimate piece). I have long since stopped feeling offended by this, realising that entertainment in its multifarious guises must start and stop with shipshape fashion in these environments. In a way, this kind of behaviour (and, indeed, wrist watches chirruping away precisely on the hour, like a chorus of recalcitrant termites), which counts as 'normal' these days, actually helps us to keep what we are doing in perspective. Cruise audiences switch you on and off as though you are responding to a remote control pointed in your direction, and I suppose that is fine: they have paid for the privilege. As a result of my experiences I now feel I could happily continue playing, even if an ice-cream van drove into the auditorium – though I once had to restart a Liszt programme at London's St John's Smith Square three times due to a CND demonstration outside. There is nothing like a bit of 'real' distraction to distract you from your own distractions.

13 Improvisation

Awakening the spontaneous you

Victor Borge once quipped that the shortest distance between two humans is laughter.[145] I would like to propose a variation: *the clearest communication between two humans is music*. When music is created, it leaps across polarities of language or age. In many cases musical communication will not stand up to verbal interrogation or amount to a direct assimilation of meaning, and yet the very act of trying in itself amounts to a kind of 'message'.

The immediacy of music is like a smile, or a tilt of the head – it tells us something we feel we understand, but cannot begin to express in words. The person next to us saw the same smile but understood it to mean something subtly different; we are less concerned with precise definitions, more interested in the power of what *seemed* to be communicated. The whole business of human communication is wonderfully imprecise and irredeemably riddled with subjectivity. It is the gaps in meaning which leave open the possibility of something unanticipated and joyful. The same, surely, is true in music.

If learning someone else's piece is a slow-burn activity, then improvising is more like spontaneous combustion. Improvisation has the power to ignite in us a spark of originality; moreover, it may help to awaken a spirit of spontaneity frequently lacking in pianists today. Somewhat incipiently, it seems to me, improvisation has been hijacked by jazz pianists during the past one hundred years or so, and while it is certainly the case that jazz players appear able to interleaf their genre very instinctively within the realm of improvisation, in truth, pianists of all persuasions would be well-advised to weave it into their skill-set, too.

Improvisation was once an entirely commonplace skill among musicians from as early as Renaissance times, and the figured bass prevalent throughout the Baroque era, or the concerto cadenza of the Classical era, are surely among the more obvious examples. The 'use it or lose it' truism undoubtedly prevails here – classically trained pianists are no longer called upon to improvise in this way, hence we no longer value it or practise it. Many diploma pianists today would struggle to play the national anthem in, say, the key of A♭ major, without dots in front of them and a dozen chances to make corrections, even though they may be able to whizz around Debussy's *Feu d'artifice* with enviable ferocity. When forced to pull out notes from our heads, even when we already know how a tune goes, we often recoil as though we have been asked to split the pianistic atom. It is not that we have forever lost this base level functionality, but simply the instinct to make confident, constructive use of it.

---

145 Victor Borge (1909–2000), Jewish-Danish comedian, conductor and pianist whose popularity throughout Europe and the USA (on TV and radio) was immeasurable.

The freedom – as distinct from fear – which can come from moving away from the printed page, can seem an enormous relief after all those hours of toiling over traditional repertoire. But first we have to let go of certain bogus beliefs and prejudices, for regrettably it seems that one way 'Classical' pianists seek to justify our lack of improvisational prowess is to demean it when it forms a central plank in someone else's musical identity. Tunnel-vision of this sort is like the serious artist who cannot abide cartoons, graffiti and pop art, or the poet who tuts cynically at the mere mention of rap. In reality, we are losing out on a fundamental component of our musical beings (not to mention heritage) when we decry such skills as secondary or barely worth the effort.

I proposed a little earlier in the book that the better skilled we become at following scores, the worse we may become at 'letting go'. Unwittingly, pianists can become hypnotised by the very presence of the score, and over a period of time easily lose that wonderfully intuitive connection with the music that even the most 'uneducated' member of an audience will undoubtedly possess. The impulse to follow our own nose (rather than allow ourselves to be led by it) and to gauge for ourselves what works and what does not, is surely a paramount skill in anyone's book? The practised improviser[146] possesses something rather valuable that the score-dependent pianist does not – a resourcefulness which comes directly from the heart in commune with the intellect; a willingness to savour the moment and delight in the possibilities of what is not yet fully known.

Just as we tend to esteem intellect over emotion, a sizeable number of pianists persist in revering the sophistications of learned repertoire over the immediacy of improvisations, jazz or otherwise. Moreover, as we learn (possibly unknowingly) to venerate the dots on the page, we inadvertently lose our capacity to listen, to respond, to experiment, to reimagine and to trust what we instinctively have to bring to the music. We forget that, without input from us, there is no music. From this perspective therefore, the straight player might well be best advised to take a leaf out of the jazz player's book.

> Mindfulness is clearly a fundamental part of jazz, and is at the core of the process of improvisation. To be truly free and 'in the moment' it is important to be able to take risks – without fear of judgment – in search of a heightened creative state. Practice plays a crucial role in preparing us to improvise, for this is where we become aware of what 'could' be played. However, in a state of mindfulness, we focus on what is being played. We resist the ideas that have arisen in our cognitive practice and seek a more immediate and intuitive space, where feeling and narrative become more important. In other words, it is possible, through practice, to acquire the eloquence to enter the world of jazz – however, the aim is to move beyond the learned vocabulary and find fresh and immediate ways of expression in the moment. **Nikki Iles**

146 This is by no means a contradiction in terms – improvisation, like any other skill, responds robustly to patient, attentive work, and is invariably best tied in with so-called 'serious' practice. Ingmar Bergman once said 'Only he who is well-prepared has any opportunity to improvise' (www.azquotes.com).

Actually, we are all improvising, all of the time, both as musicians and in our daily lives as we collide with others on the tube or laugh at something we said quite by accident. Yet, frustratingly perhaps, our ordered lives seem to stifle our willingness to relish serendipity – we worry about the consequences of getting lost in an unknown city, or what might happen if we dare to sit next to a stranger in Starbucks. What hope, then, for the modern day pianist ridden with hang-ups and eager to rekindle a little freestyle spontaneity in their playing?

The pianist who embraces improvisation relishes uncertainty, for among the jangle of notes that dribble mischievously from the fingers may lie four golden notes or a single open-ended chord (Tristan?) worthy of closer scrutiny. Soon something rather intriguing and wonderful seems in prospect. The sheer amusement and amazement of invention, and of miraculous chance discovery, supersedes virtually any amount of satisfaction gained from running with someone else's idea or someone else's brainchild, even if it happens to have come from Beethoven.

I asked Harry The Piano to coin the essence of cabaret improvisation for me. He said this:

> The question I'm most often asked after a performance improvising on audience requests is 'what on earth is going on in your head?' Reinterpreting the melody of a song, film theme or the like, as if imagined by Mozart, Liszt or Satie, is all a matter of immersion in the various styles – and I mean *immersion*. Learning to improvise first involves learning to listen with serious intensity, in the way an actor might aurally immerse him/herself when preparing for a role with an accent other than their own. So what makes Mozart sound like Mozart? If you listen to enough, you begin to absorb the basics of Alberti bass, the placement of accented passing notes (or passing chords), creating tiny moments of tension and resolution, his voicings, cadence patterns and the shape of his melodic lines. When eventually you have learned to speak with a Mozartian accent, as it were, *it makes no difference what you are asked to say.* Harry The Piano, AKA Harry Harris

Improvisation is not a panacea for all pianistic ills, but it can be immensely illuminating and rejuvenating, especially for pianists who feel they have lost a little of the wonderment and hutzpah they once had in their piano playing. I am not advocating a 'cold turkey' approach to learning from scores here, or a rejection of what it means to have a Rachmaninov prelude immaculately under your fingers, for this is a thing of wonder, too. Rather, I am encouraging a more balanced understanding of the role our subconscious can have in concert with our conscious mind; improvisation brings us into closer contact with our inventive personas and can reignite in us a passion for sound, instinct and emotion, all of which is surely central to the very creation of any kind of music.

Finding the method in our madness

I have always rejected the widely-held notion that we cannot be 'wrong' when we are improvising: the idiom(s) we are working with will nearly always require us to reference certain touchstones regularly in order for it to 'work' plausibly. Granted, the true benefits of learning to improvise have little to do with what others may think about it – improvisation is not obliged to be a spectator sport, after all[147] – and yet there is surely a great deal more to successful improvising than playing a long, meandering chain of notes which eventually come to a merciful halt after a randomly gauged period of time. Of course the improviser has the power to move with the tide – and have fun – but not at any cost.

I believe that although we all embrace innovation in music, we also long for orderliness. Spontaneity comes at a price – for it to work, we need to be ready to relax our grip on the 'known', even momentarily. 'Systems' in music function as the pillars around which spontaneity drapes itself. Without structure, we lack the framework for imagining the existence of something quirky or unexpected. Structures are there to give order and shape to what would otherwise remain disparate, unconnected ideas. Although the 'rules' are ours to make, and ours to modify when we see fit, there *are* rules. Expert improvisers draw from an instinctive awareness of how to unfold a musical story, just as wordsmiths appear able to accord a satisfying rhythmic status to every sentence they utter – there's always a beginning, middle and end. Without necessarily realising it, it is the value we place in a piece of music's architectural signposts which we are most fearful of losing – the composer takes the guesswork out of the music's trajectory on a macro scale, leaving us free to have fun piecing together the micro-moments. Our willingness to make musical decisions on a bar-by-bar basis depends directly upon the certainty that more music is to be found printed on the next page; few of us would have the mettle to continue under our own steam just for the fun of it; we would probably just stop, scratch our head and get on with something else.

A chief fringe-benefit of feeling confident in improvising is that we can focus much more on *sound* – we learn to zone in on the subtlest nuances of our melodic, harmonic and rhythmic playing, of pedalling, balance and chord-voicing, and the most atmospheric or intense musical message we are capable of drawing out from within us and our instrument. Pianists have to work a little harder than, say, a cellist when attempting to keep in touch with the beauty of our sound. The cellist feels every part of the resonant sound coursing through their veins – they are not *making* the sound, they *are* the sound. I love the tactility of the piano – how it feels under my fingers, the tiniest variants of ivory between certain keys, even the chipped edge on that high G – but I do envy those who can alter the effect of each note by adding vibrato or taking it away, blending in a more yearning intensity by *crescendo*-ing through it – all on the spur of the moment.

147 Twyla Tharp said 'It's you alone, with no one watching or judging. If anything comes of it, you decide whether the world gets to see it. In essence, you are giving yourself permission to daydream during working hours.' (www.goodreads.com)

Improvisation has the power to unleash all kinds of musical instincts in us which we otherwise might keep under lock and key. For us to be mindful in learning a piece by Debussy, we first need to know what emotional magic lives inside us, and this means knowing both ourselves and our instrument, being free with what both have to offer and feeling empowered to access these whenever our playing calls for it. A willingness to take risks is the engine of our spontaneity, and we may be surprised to hear just how much our Beethoven playing improves when we become more resourceful at improvising in the style of Borodin or Miles Davis.

Once improvising has become a regular part of our piano playing, we find ourselves stumbling across an Aladdin's cave of possibilities every time we sit down to play. The point is not to turn ourselves into expert improvisers, but to refuel the bank of resources we delve into every time we 'retell' the story of a Mozart sonata or Chopin nocturne. Strangely, the liberating feeling we get when we allow ourselves to explore an inner world of minimalist harmonies or obscure rhythms can actually broaden our palette of possibilities when we next sit down to play Handel. When we improvise, we get to meet ourselves coming back from another direction. Hence the true value in becoming secure as improvisers lies not in the ability to impress others in a wine bar, but in the potential to release an impulse for genuine innovation we scarcely imagined was there at all.

Going loopy

A hazard of improvising is that we can all too easily end up looping around a familiar shape or progression.[148] Instead of nurturing something that sounds new and exciting, we find ourselves revisiting pre-rehearsed strategies, for example turning the corner into the home key. Our improvisation sessions slip alarmingly into repetitive sequences from which it seems impossible to extricate ourselves.[149] We feel powerless to resist the magnetic pull of a comfortable hand shape or a chromatically descending bass line. It is as if we are compelled by some force outside of ourselves to go through a groundhog-day experience each time we sit down to improvise, no matter what we start by doing.

For these reasons I now offer a few triggers for your improvising to nudge you away from the well-trodden path.

Triggers

- Start with a key you are less comfortable with; quarantine any key you naturally gravitate towards.

- Borrow from a piece you already know well – find an interesting chord-pairing and work it into a succinct repeating figure; from here you can begin to piece together a melody, and a whole vista of possibilities opens up before your very ears.

---

148 I believe it was Count Basie who said that 'the best improvisations are well-rehearsed.'
149 Sheila Heti once said 'True improvisation is about surprising yourself – but most people won't improvise truthfully. They're afraid. What they do is pull from their bag of tricks. They take what they already know how to do and apply it to the present situation.' (www.topfamousquotes.com)

- Create your own concerto cadenza using fragments borrowed from a classical sonata you happen to be working on. Stitch your ideas together by whatever bold key transformations, shifts in register or texture and changes of metre you feel are necessary. You may well find you are more 'alive' when you come to play that sonata next time.

- Overcome any prejudice you may have against dissonance. The piano is surprisingly forgiving of notes which lie outside the immediate confines of a given key, especially if you physically widen the gap between them; use the pedal with confidence and go with where your improvisation seems to want to go. Try moving from consonant to dissonant notes/chords and back again; enjoy not quite knowing what you have created. 'Rude' harmonies almost invariably turn out to be more loaded with potential than 'polite' ones.

- Move away from the middle of the piano to avoid feeling ring-fenced. By separating the hands by three, four or even five octaves, we find ourselves working with new versions/incarnations of well-worn harmonies. If we dare to move both hands up or down the keyboard, generously supported by pedal, we can ease ourselves into an intriguing, more fantastical sound-world.

- Jot down ideas on the back of an envelope and keep it on your lap as you improvise. Glance down at it when you need to, but resist for as long as you dare.

- Don't hop about too much with your ideas. The 'less is more' philosophy undeniably holds good in profitable improvising. Spend as long as you need before discovering an idea you like, then stick with it and invest time in it. Coax it, finesse it, transpose it, invert it, re-harmonise it, extend it...

- Stretching intervals is a time-honoured approach to taking your melodic ideas on an enjoyable journey. Simply take your improvised melody and find the biggest interval within it; then make it bigger by one or more steps.

- Look for sequences and patterns in what you have just produced. Even if there appears to be no obvious shape to what you have come up with, chances are that with a bit of imagination you can find a way to extend twenty seconds of music into three minutes' worth.

- Sequences are the opposite of repetitions – repetitions are useful to emphasise and reinforce, but they do not take ideas further forward. As soon as you are able to generate some kind of directional 'pull' within your idea, it is off and running. Now try moving the sequence wholesale, perhaps in progressive intervals of a fourth, quasi Bach.

- Don't forget your left hand. We tend to be so right-hand dominant when improvising that we overlook the extraordinary powers of the left hand, not just as a provider of accompanimental figures, but as a colouristic tool and indeed as an able ambassador of melodies. Often an improvisation is rendered impotent simply because there is no viable texture or accompaniment to prop it up. Why not start with a few accompanimental shapes, keeping the hand as 'still' as is possible, while moving smoothly from one harmonic shape to the next.

- The augmentation and diminution of an idea, be it harmonic or melodic, is another tool widely used by composers to expand upon a relatively simple pattern. Take a simple four-chord trick (say, I IV V I) and splice in some 'new' chords in between each one.

- Try not to get angry or frustrated with yourself when nothing original is forthcoming. Move away from the instrument, make a cup of tea and stroke the cat; then go back and improvise the best music you have ever played.

- As soon as you feel stale, it is time to try something else. Staleness leads to impoverished intuition, which in turn leads inevitably back to looping the loop. Improvising should never be an absent-minded activity – we want to feel we are flying by the seat of our pants in a direction not yet decided upon. Do something dramatic with your feet perhaps – see how the pedals can affect what you were just doing – or move to an extreme dynamic (playing as softly as you dare can be a fantastically refreshing way of triggering an entirely new atmosphere).

- Record yourself improvising – not all of the time, but when you feel particularly in the mood.

- Be aware of what you just did, then do it again. Originality is most realistically measured over a longer period of time, not necessarily in the space of two minutes. Whereas we need to be brave enough to reject ideas that seem limp or legless, we need to be bold and assertive with those ideas which have the potential to evolve.

- Take the metronome and crank up the pace. Inexperienced drummers often seem to be capable of playing in just two speeds – 'fast' and 'slow' – and we pianists all too easily migrate back to our comfortable (frequently slow) tempo also. If we allow ourselves to inhabit a particular pace all of the time, we will inevitably find ourselves reliving a mood or 'energy' that is already well known to us; from here, true innovation is made inestimably harder.[150]

- Be adventurous with your harmonic progressions; nothing needs to be off limits unless your ears tell you otherwise. Dare to play a strange F♯ major-type chord after C major; experiment with added notes – the added 2nd, 4th, 6th and major 7th are your best friends when it comes to keeping your harmonies headed in a direction of your own choosing (whereas the dominant 7th wants to 'pull' you to its tonic, which may not be where you are ready to return just yet).

- Try wholesale shifting of a familiar piece/melody that was originally in a major key into a minor, or vice versa – an exceptional way of 'disguising' it![151]

150 Patti Smith: 'It's like drumming. If you miss a beat, you create another.' (www.goodreads.com)
151 I am reminded of an enlightening Q&A given by Harry The Piano in the company of Murray McLachlan at Chetham's International Piano Summer School in 2015 – if I recall correctly, Harry successfully camouflaged Tom Jones's *Delilah* by switching its tonality and giving it a sort of French waltz 'feel', thereby rendering it undetected by 99% of those present (including me).

- Finally, try improvising with a fellow pianist. One of you could be generating some kind of harmonic direction in the lower/middle register, while the other responds and feeds back ideas from the higher register.

Visual triggers

The power of visualisation for musicians can be considerable. If a picture paints a thousand words, it can coax out any number of musical ideas from an alert mind. Images, illustrations, remembered scenes from films[152] and even cartoons,[153] can be used very effectively to trigger piano improvisations.[154] These are even more open-ended than musical stimuli, which to some extent always come 'preloaded'. Even an out-of-focus photograph, taken on the fly, has the capacity to suggest a tentative narrative, while a collage can function as an elaborate visual storyboard to encourage a more ambitious improvisation. The beauty of using images in this way is that they are everywhere around us; furthermore, we all relate to them in personal ways, and indeed a particular picture might trigger an entirely original musical chain of events upon successive encounters. The connection between a picture and its perceived meaning becomes all the more palpable when coupled with a spirited, improvised musical event.

For the piano teacher, using visual triggers can prove a tremendous fillip in lessons when the river runs dry. Whether at the level of beginner or advanced, a pianist can spend valuable time engaged in this way, perhaps using a florid passage borrowed from a piece by Ravel to combine with a photograph of a gothic church window, or a crazy animal image to stimulate a humorous improvisation 'vignette'. Because improvisations are by their very definition amorphous and pliable, they foster a responsiveness to the here and now, especially perhaps as regards 'static' images; all permutations remain entirely at the whim of the player. I have enjoyed using the bizarre symbolic paintings of Hieronymus Bosch[155] and Salvador Dalí[156] as improvisation triggers for many years; they seem to unlock a vault of mysterious, fantastical thoughts in players of any age.

The example on page 116 is a painting entitled 'Rust Belt'.[157] Its intriguing melange of indeterminate shades might even allude to a chromatic run of black and white piano keys, while its bold parallel vertical structures offer the pianist

152 The British pianist, John Lenehan (born 1961) has taken the art of arranging and improvising music for movies to an impressively high level.
153 I have found Simon's Cat to be a terrific online resource for characterful improvisation, not exclusively with youngsters, because each cartoon lasts just long enough to stimulate ideas which recur – a *glissando* to suggest sliding down a stairway perhaps, quiet *staccato* notes in the bass to portray something impending, or an explosive chord using the extremes of the keyboard to convey a chest of drawers crashing to the ground. https://simonscat.com
154 Furthermore, the value of off-the-cuff pictorial analogies – which I find myself using frequently in my teaching and writing – often strikes home more accessibly than direct musical references when giving deliberations to contestants at music festivals.
155 Early Netherlandish painter (c.1450–1516).
156 Spanish surrealist painter and multi-collaborator (1904–1989).
157 The British artist, Harriet Poznansky (born 1990), presented this painting as a trigger for improvisation at a lecture I gave on behalf of EPTA at Yamaha Music London, 2014. 'Rust Belt' (January 2013) is painted with oil, ink, graphite and silver pigment on cotton. Dimensions: 75 x 55 cm.

multiple possibilities for working with both texture (block chords, perhaps) and even timescale (regular intervals or markers).[158] The physical dimensions of the painting will necessarily impact on the improviser differently when viewed full-size on a gallery wall, though even in this graphic representation we immediately see the possibilities for improvising and experimenting with mood, tone-colour, light and shade, soft and loud, slow and fast. The blurred, shadowy lines, which crisscross the painting so vividly, might invite the pianist to contemplate an adventurous palette of pedal effects (*sostenuto* could be especially effective to depict the rogue 'cross-stroke'), while use of register in response to the painting's range of ghostlike hues could prove especially featureful for the improviser. It is the process of re-constituting all these visual elements using imaginative *musical* language that is of principle value here, and indeed the discussion between players, or between teacher and pupil, that it can stimulate. Though the temporal imperative of an improvisation must always lie in stark contrast with the fixedness of the painting, this itself could prove a valuable topic for discussion – how might an improvisation encapsulate the visual and physical proportions of the painting in real time? The faintest suggestion of flower petals scattered along the left of the painting could provoke some enterprising musical detail within an improvisation too, as might its absence of frame, seemingly keeping it unconstrained, or even the 'woody' texture resulting from the confident single brush-strokes out of which the painting springs to life. Feeling free to use the instrument as an interface between the image and the musical response it triggers gives a whole new meaning to the term 'performance art'; hence, with a little encouragement, visual representations can open up a cornucopia of sounds lying dormant even in a relatively inexperienced player.

Know your instrument

As a suffix to improvising, and as we near the end of the book, I cannot quite bring myself to close off without making brief mention of something I feel we generally take for granted; our instrument. For all its powers, the piano cannot be mindful of itself; we have to be mindful on its behalf. The piano might be capable of producing an unquantifiable number of sounds, and its action easily dismissed as a mere mechanism, yet it is so much more than a 'sound machine'. In much of our day-to-day piano playing, we act as though our instrument is something which needs to be 'operated' or 'managed' – we talk of learning to 'control' it, we perform and play 'on' it, we improvise 'at' it and in so many other ways we presume to impose our will; like the lion tamer and the lion. But this is a rather one-dimensional view, which underestimates the closer kinship which ideally should evolve over time between the piano and its player.

If I could change one single aspect of what pianists do when sat at the piano, it would be to encourage us all to be more aware of how the piano makes its sound, and what actually causes different musical effects to come out of it.

---

158   The picture was intended to be viewed in landscape mode, though arguably an entirely new set of possibilities comes from turning the image through a series of 90° angles.

View from this angle

'Rust Belt' © Harriet Poznansky, 2013

We are the source of the sound, and therefore the music, whereas the piano – until coaxed from its sleep – is just a rather fantastic looking piece of furniture that is the envy (or perhaps the cause of torment) of our neighbours.

Let me offer you one very small exercise to help strengthen the bond between you and your instrument involving our old friend, the sustain pedal. Most of us use it and abuse it, but have you ever stopped to consider what the pedal actually does? Of course we all know about sympathetic vibration, damper action and so on, but that is not really what I am getting at. The next time you sit at the piano, and before you have played a note of your Bartók, play your favourite chord in your favourite key. With the pedal already down, play a large, majestic chord – a real 'waaa' attack, not a 'dit' – with the hands spaced far apart, and just listen to what happens. In fact, since you have the pedal down, play several loud chords ensuring notes from all registers of the piano get trapped in the pedalled sound. Sit back and listen to it ring out. After just a few brief seconds, even on an excellent grand with the lid up, the highest notes will have completely disappeared.[159] Count a few more seconds, and notes from an octave lower will have begun to dwindle. Ten seconds later we are only really hearing the bass-tenor register plus the last vestiges of overtones from higher up. It could be a further forty seconds to a minute, or more, before the sound has truly disappeared, and when it has it will be the lowest notes you played which lingered the longest.

If only we could be a little more aware of this characteristic when we apply the pedal routinely in Brahms or Tchaikovsky, we would be so much more in resonance (literally) with our instrument. Putting the subtleties of half-pedalling to one side, we will have come a little closer to knowing when we need to use pedal and when we would be better off giving it a wide berth (even, exceptionally, when the score indicates otherwise).

From this simple exercise we can see that music which is orientated predominantly around the middle (and indeed lower) register will likely need even more care as regards pedal than music in which both hands are working above the middle of the instrument.[160] For a huge number of piano pieces, from all eras, a combination of efficient finger-pedalling and finger-substitution (quasi the organist), complemented with judicious dabs of pedal strictly where needed, will get the job done admirably.

---

159 Piano technicians know that the life of the top notes is so short the piano does not even need dampers in that region.
160 The second movement of Beethoven's *Pathètique* would be an excellent example, but actually this will be true of much 18th and early 19th century repertoire.

14 The virtuoso listener

We all know virtuosity when we hear it. Virtuosity lives on a pinhead where fallible humanity and otherworldliness miraculously collide. Though we can perhaps barely grasp what we are hearing, or indeed watching, we feel strangely drawn to others who demonstrate a capacity to live on the cusp of impossibility. One of my first experiences of feeling awestricken by a performance was upon listening to Ivo Pogorelich's recording of Schumann's *Toccata*. We automatically sit up and take notice when something singularly charismatic and utterly 'in the zone' seems to be taking place. While most of us know we may never be capable of such feats ourselves, we take vicarious pride in what our species can achieve when everything comes together so miraculously.

Virtuosity, then, would appear to be all about the *execution* of something rather marvellous. But virtuosos do not appear out of a puff of stardust; the teacher invariably plays a substantial role.[161] Paul Harris, in his much-lauded book, *The Virtuoso Teacher*, takes an interesting slip road from the theme of virtuosity.[162] In a nutshell, Harris also wants us to aspire to a comparable level of mastery in our teaching.[163] Today, virtuoso piano teachers wander down many of the corridors of the top conservatoires, yet few will ever achieve what Heinrich Neuhaus (and others would argue, Fanny Waterman) managed in one lifetime. But, along with teaching, it seems to me yet another viable 'B road' of virtuosity is worth considering: *the virtuoso listener*. Once the teaching has been done, and the performing is unfolding, something else quite astonishing needs to happen inside the listener's head, or it all becomes a little meaningless and self-congratulatory: our minds and hearts need to be worthy conduits of the music.

In order to develop something close to virtuosic listening skills, first we need to appreciate that listening and understanding are wholly different things. So many times I have heard people (even seasoned pianists) say things like 'I just don't *understand* that piece.' I always feel slightly baffled by this – surely there is nothing to 'understand' as such? We do not feel the need to understand the taste of a banana, or the aroma of a wild flower. We can like a piece, or not, but either way, we are not being invited by the composer to understand the piece, merely to give it a chance.[164] What goes on between our ears is wonderfully mysterious, and ultimately perhaps not anyone else's business.

---

161 There was a day (probably just before his second birthday) when even Mozart could not read or play music.

162 Harris, P., 2012: *The Virtuoso Teacher* (London, Faber).

163 We only have to look at the enviable student roster of Heinrich Neuhaus (1888–1964), himself a pupil of Godowsky, whose reputation as a 'virtuoso piano teacher' seems almost beyond compare. Neuhaus's pupils included Radu Lupu, Sviatoslav Richter and Emil Gilels.

164 A person who can listen supremely in a piano exam, for example, and harness this skill when performing to an exceptional level, may actually fall down conspicuously in the aural component of the same exam. There is no contradiction here at all – indeed, in my experience this happens rather frequently.

A listener does not necessarily need expert knowledge to function at a virtuosic level, though it is essential to have a heightened receptivity to 'sensation' and a sensitivity to what music amounts to in purely aesthetic, experiential terms.[165] The virtuoso listener exists everywhere, in the car, in the supermarket, even in the gym. Only we will ever know whether we have sharpened our qualities of listening to a point where we feel we can resonate with the music at its core, elemental level. When we are touched by a musical experience – not necessarily by the words a singer happens to be singing, for example – and completely in resonance with what it means for us, we can feel free to upgrade ourselves to the status of virtuoso listener.

> It is possible to perform a piece without listening intently to the result, but could we be hearing what we *want* to hear, rather than the sounds actually being produced? Let us ask ourselves questions as we play: is the architecture clearly pinpointed (e.g. the recapitulation, shifts of tonality, or repeats, which divert into new territory)? Is the balance and voicing adjusted to delineate where the melody lies, without being sabotaged by a heavy-handed accompaniment or muddy pedalling? Is each phrase on a journey to and from its apex, so that it acquires a sense of purpose? **Nancy Litten**

Teachers often worry that listening to recordings when learning a piece is dangerous because we may inadvertently pick up the inflections as well as the more fundamental habits of that performer. This, the argument runs, may serve to shut down our willingness to experiment and to judge for ourselves what is likely to work best. I have always been a quiet dissenter of this view. Many of the pieces we learn as more advanced players were chosen *precisely* because we 'know' it well already, and may have heard it performed on countless occasions. Our love affair with the piece has to begin somewhere. The alternative is for pianists to go through a series of 'blind date' experiences, never quite knowing whether we are embarking upon something new and exciting, or simply squandering valuable time.

Granted, once we have successfully moved beyond the formative stages of learning a piece, and have become engaged with it in the ways I have been encouraging the reader to try in the book, we need to be brave enough to move away from admired recordings. It is only at this point, I would suggest, that a risk of becoming side-tracked may indeed arise. But, in and of itself, I firmly believe we pianists should get on with evolving our listening skills to the level of virtuoso and then wait for our fingers to catch up. Without this indispensable *yearning* to play a piece, which in many cases will come from hearing it played rather beautifully by someone else, we are depriving ourselves of an essential form of inspiration and motivation.

---

165 A good chef continually seasons and tastes before sending food out from the kitchen. In the same way, the pianist must always be listening, monitoring and making infinitesimal alterations.

Listen with new ears

Enjoy the sensation of listening to a new piano piece every day. I got into the habit of doing this while at college, usually sat in the library with headphones on as I sipped my afternoon tea. Over the period of a typical graduate course, you might realistically add close to one thousand pieces to your knowledge bank by this method; from these, there may be thirty that stimulate you sufficiently to roll your sleeves up and learn the music. Savour the newness of the experience and delight in the music's unforeseen turns. Be as random as you like in your trawl, certainly not chronological (or in any other way logical), though try to keep a note of what you have heard. Allow each piece to wash over you in a single gulp; drink it in and keep it. The experience you are having is yours to do with as you wish. Try to resist the impulse to evaluate, and do not become unduly concerned with how certain effects may have been achieved or notated. Indeed, I would advise not having the score in front of you at this stage; the machinery of the piece can have its moment later. Just be happy to have discovered something of beauty. Let it fuel your imagination.

Childs' play

Here is a musical 'game' you can have fun with, while simultaneously giving your brain a workout.[166] Take any melody you know inside out and play it through in an easy key a couple of times, just to get it firmly into your fingers. Now, as you begin to play it once more, break it down into its composite phrases, bars, or alternatively places where the music pauses to breathe naturally, but instead of continuing on with what you know to be the right note, restart at the pitch you just *arrived* at. This effectively forces you to transpose the melody a number of times in a single sitting. The musical effect is quite absurd, since you will of course invariably end up in an entirely unrelated key, but that is the fun of it. Variants on this might include starting in a more difficult key and seeing where you end up, or adding the harmony too, which will doubtless stretch even the most adept Harry The Piano emulators.

It is probably easier to give an example. *Good King Wenceslas* appears opposite, firstly as we know and love it, and then debauched for our own mindful purposes!

---

166 I am indebted to the eponymous Marilyn Childs (whose father apparently invented this 'musical game' to keep the children quiet in the back of the car on long journeys) for sharing it with me while attending one of my annual Piano Summer Schools at Jackdaws, in Frome, Somerset: www.jackdaws.co.uk

Good King Wenceslas

15 The mindful non-pianist

It is entirely possible that your love for the piano stems from concert-going, listening to recordings, reading reviews or from a fascination for the instrument itself, rather than as a practitioner. Astute observations frequently come from observers on piano courses, masterclasses and music-appreciation events, and it is gratifying to see how many mindful non-pianists feel moved to take up the challenge and learn to play. The piano is surely among the more approachable of instruments – approachable in its more literal sense, for we can simply stroll up to one when nobody is looking and tinkle a few keys, just to satisfy a fleeting moment's curiosity. Importantly, we cannot do this with a trumpet, violin or flute. Indeed, an untrained person can derive immediate pleasure from making sounds on the piano and hearing them reverberate around a room. Everything is laid bare on a piano keyboard – it begs to be played. Its geography, as we like to call it, which is set out in alternating groups of two and three black keys to aid orientation, is interspersed with a run of white keys marshalled from top to bottom. If you have never tried, I would urge you to experience the joy of playing; you might get the bug. It hardly matters that your initial contact will seem random in the sense that you are simply responding to impulses over which you have little control. The piano's tactility was what you were probably first drawn to, so just give in to it.

Here are a few little exercises pitched at the complete newcomer – you might wish to try these for yourself if you happen to have access to a half-decent instrument (or indeed a touch-sensitive electric keyboard) over the course of a week or two. Chapter 3, *Connecting your mind with your body*, would be an excellent way to inaugurate your learning. By the end of this brief 'primer' you can say, with a straight face, that you are a pianist.

1 Sit squarely at the piano with your belly button twelve to fifteen inches from the keyhole, and place your right hand somewhere near the right half of the piano. For now, just use your index and middle fingers (these being the strongest), and explore the feel of the white and black keys, paying particular attention to those in close proximity to each other. It is with these that you may, with a little perseverance, be able to pick out a tune you know well. You can join notes together smoothly and effectively, simply by watching and listening intently to how they slightly 'overlap', thus making a pleasurable approximation of your tune in a matter of a minute or two. Use other fingers if you feel confident enough, but in any case aim to keep the hand relaxed and 'claw-like' in shape in order to retain close contact with the keys. Though the tune may conceivably require you to use one or more black keys in order to sound 'right', for the present, always start on a white key. If you can get close to coaxing out the tune – which in many cases will be achievable using the notes contained within a single octave or so – have a go at playing it with the left hand somewhere lower down on the keyboard, just for the fun of it. You will doubtless discover how any tune you come up with

will map out anywhere on the keyboard, just as long as you reposition your hand in relation to the same starting note. You will also quickly spot that the fingers you use to pick out the tune in the left hand will be the mirror-image of those you would use in the right hand; herein lies one of the fundamental conundrums of piano playing, for as soon as we attempt to play the same tune in both hands simultaneously we are effectively having to split our mind into two as we attempt to neatly align the right thumb with the left little finger, for example.

2 Now, using your right foot, press down the right pedal (regardless of how many pedals the piano happens to have) and try playing your tune again. Depending on how high or low you happen to be on the keyboard, you will find that the pedal has created varying degrees of 'muddle', which should immediately prompt you to lift the pedal in order to clear the sound from its 'memory bank', then depress it again immediately afterwards. With your left hand, using your index and ring fingers, experiment with a few two-note chords (white keys only at first, keeping all chords as close together as possible) nice and softly, somewhere to the left of centre on the keyboard. Depress the pedal as you do so and listen intently to notice how the sound appears appreciably 'warmer'. Were you to play two adjacent chords *without* changing the pedal (i.e. lifting and depressing it again), the blurring effect may not please you, so see whether you are able to use the pedal more discriminately by changing it a fraction of a second *after* you play each successive chord.

3 The fun really begins when you attempt to play tunes and chords simultaneously – quite a feat of coordination at this formative stage. Be patient with yourself and see whether you are able to align your chords with your tune – resist the urge to change the chord with every new note you play – in many cases a chord will work perfectly well for several melody notes at a time. Finding which chords work effectively with the melody notes will, by necessity, require trial and error, but will be all the more satisfying as you slowly discover which ones work well together. Adding pedal may initially seem a huge additional challenge, but stick with it, and over a period of perhaps a few days of playing for short, concentrated periods of time, you may be able to combine the tune, chords and pedal quite plausibly. Piano playing is as simple or complex as you choose to make it, but savour the simple pleasure of listening to sounds *you* have been able to create.[167]

4 I have so far deliberately neglected to mention two rather important things, mainly because I wanted you to discover these for yourself. Pianists can fundamentally only control two things when we play: how *loud* notes sound, and *how long* they last. The first is determined by the force we apply,[168] the second is simply a function of how long we choose to keep keys pressed down once we have played them (the sustain pedal can achieve this with

---

167 If you can drive a car with manual gears, you should in theory be able to learn to play the piano. When we stop to think of it, it is primarily our *ears* which we use to gauge when to change gear.
168 See footnote 25 for further clarification of this important point.

multiple notes, as you have doubtless figured out for yourself). When one hand plays louder than the other, we get a rather special balance effect, which becomes increasingly important to cultivate as we go on to more complex playing. Enjoy experimenting with the extremities of the keyboard too, either with or without the aid of pedal, and with or without the other hand playing notes at the same time. Nothing is off-limits – the more adventurous you are, the quicker you will learn what your instrument is capable of, and expand the range of possibilities open to you.

5 When you have grown in confidence at combining both hands and your right foot, why not see whether you can create a short murder-mystery improviastion, making especial use of the middle and bass notes – or perhaps something more ethereal, enjoying the rather special effect produced by the very top notes. When you experiment with the hands placed rather further apart you will find a gamut of possibilities opens up for you – it will initially be more profitable to create 'effects', not 'tunes' *per se*. Be really confident with the pedals (feel free to introduce the *una corda* – left pedal – whenever you are wanting a more muted effect), and see how far you can push the envelope as regards the range and qualities of the sounds you make.[169]

This has been something of a crash course, but imagine what you might achieve if you were to stick at playing for a month or more. In the fullness of time you will inevitably wish to equip yourself with one of the many excellent adult tutor books available, but notice that I have consciously avoided all references to note names, time-values, key-signatures and all other theoretical elements; aim not to become preoccupied with reading music during the first few months of learning from scratch.[170] The currency of music is sound, not paper; our ears tend to switch off when we stare unflinchingly at the page, and as I have stated time and again within these pages, it is the kinship you feel with the instrument that should remain your top priority. I do hope I have whetted your appetite, and that you will wish to continue exploring and expressing yourself as you continue learning to play the piano. Perhaps you recently inherited a rather beautiful older instrument, or feel an irresistible urge to splash out on one. Why not get rid of that vase and doily, get the thing tuned and let a little piano playing into your life?

169 Every instrument – even a woodworm-ridden century-old upright – possesses its own special spectrum of possibilities. But these amount to nothing unless the player applies his/her imagination in pursuit of every scintilla of colour and effect.
170 Although it is certainly the case that far more tutor books are pitched at children than adults, you might take a look at Carol Barratt's *The Classic Piano Course* (Omnibus Press), Christopher Norton's *Microjazz for Complete Beginners* (Boosey & Hawkes), Michael Aaron's *Adult Piano Course* Book 1 (Belwin) and the *Hal Leonard Piano Method*, Books 1 and 2. Many teachers take the view that we ought not to worry unduly about whether a tutor is aimed at youngsters or adults, and that we should simply concern ourselves with how systematic the approach is.

Postlude

Writing this book has been something of a catharsis. When we have all the time in the world to think and reflect, it seems we feel disinclined, instead choosing to get on with cluttering up next year's diary or looking for the cat food. But when a publisher's deadline looms, the brain leaps into gear and the subject in hand quickly consumes every waking minute. You find yourself rushing away from the hotel bellboy in order to write down some random thought you just had about chromatic scales, and turning into that comical fixture who has taken up residence in Starbucks at 6:30 each morning, armed with two laptops and a double-cappuccino.

A book of this size cannot possibly aspire to more than scratch the surface of what it is to be, or become, a more mindful pianist (or indeed, a more mindful *non*-pianist). But it has, I hope, at least opened the mind to some of the things we might do to bring a bit of order and common sense to the time we spend enjoying the company of our beloved instrument. In trying to choose one final point to leave the reader with, I decided to come back to something mentioned in passing by Philip Fowke in his Foreword: 'practice makes permanent.' The old adage that 'practice makes perfect' is well-intended, and there are surely worse notions to have rattling around in our heads if it spurs us on to work harder at something; but actually, nothing I have ever practised has made it remotely near to being perfect. Of one thing we can be pretty confident however – if we work things over enough times, they will tend to stick. But these include the things we wish we could expunge too, such as bearing down on the keys with the weight of the world on our shoulders, or beating ourselves up for stuttering six times in the *stretto* of a fugue, as well as those habits we are quietly pleased to have installed successfully onto our hard drives. To an extent, we must live with what we were born with, yet I have always despised that overworked/fatuous word, 'talent'.[171]

It is also true that we should dare to reinvent ourselves as pianists (maybe more than once), and pursue enjoyment with even greater determination as we sit down to play Fauré's *Dolly Suite* with a good friend for the hundredth time. For many of us, retirement will consume anything up to half of our lives, so we need to fill that void with positive experiences. No one can climb into our heads and sort out the dodgy bits of wiring for us; we will have to do that for ourselves.[172] My take home message is simply this: if we set ourselves up to fail, we certainly will, but if we plan to succeed, and make it possible to achieve something rather marvellous, we just might.

---

171 Living with what we were born with is a central theme in Atarah Ben-Tovim's book: Ben-Tovim, A., and Boyd, D., [2012 reprint]: *The Right Instrument for your Child* (Orion Press).
172 You have the potential to exceed the expectations others may have of you; first, you must surpass yourself.